Islam 2000

1st Edition
(1417 A.H. / 1996 A.C.)

2nd Revised Edition
(1418 A.H./1997 A.C.)

Islam 2000

Murad Hofmann

amana publications
Beltsville, Maryland
1418/1997

amana publications
10710 Tucker Street
Beltsville, Maryland 20705-2223 USA
Tel: (301) 595-5777 Fax: (301) 595-5888
E-mail: amana@igprinting.com, www.amana-publications.com

Library of Congress Cataloging-in-Publication Data

Hofmann, Murad Wilfried (1931) —
Islam 2000
Murad Wilfried Hofmann

p. 80 cm. 15 x 23

ISBN 0-915957-70-1

1. Islam--20th century. I. Title.

BP163.H64 1996

96-38162
CIP

Printed in the United States of America by International Graphics
10710 Tucker Street
Beltsville, Maryland 20705-2223 USA
Tel. (301) 595-5999 Fax (301) 595-5888
E-mail: amana@igprinting.com

Contents

Preface

This is not the first book I have written on the subject of Islam. My previous books had, however, mainly been addressed to non-Muslims. The present booklet, on the other hand, has been written for my fellow Muslims. In describing where the Muslim world is at the threshold of the twenty-first century and what it takes to make Islam the relevant religion for that century—worldwide—I had to be severely critical of both the Occident and the Muslim world.

If I am able to offer something, it is perhaps realism. Brutal realism some readers may say. But I hope that such readers, too, will realize how much I suffer myself under the highlighted shortcomings. I am, however, convinced that concerned Muslims—jolted out of lethargy, complacency, self-doubt, and their traditional apologetic mentality, will bring about the rejuvenation of God's religion we all hope for. For the sake of mankind.

Murad Wilfried Hofmann
Istanbul, 1995/1416

CHAPTER 1

A Bit of Muslim Futurology

On 24 Ramadan 1420 A.H., with cheers or anguish, the world at large will celebrate the beginning of the third millennium after Christ. The Muslims, too, on that 1 January 2000 C.E. may have reason to ponder what is in store for them even while Muslim futurology, in this respect, seems to be of little help.

Indeed, depending on his personal temperament and experiences in life, a Muslim may well feel that Islam is, and has been, in constant decline ever since the first generation of Muslims lived in al Madinah al Munawwarah. Did the Prophet not warn us that every generation after him would be less trustworthy?[1] Al Bukhārī, in the "Book of Afflictions" (88) of his *Ṣaḥīḥ* collected many dire predictions, including the saying of the Prophet that "no time will come but the time following it will be worse than it."[2] Another Muslim might see history in waves, as a series of ups and downs, advancing, if at all, in a spiral. A third Muslim, obviously an optimist, may feel entitled to perceive Islam as making constant linear progress.

Each of these three Muslims could ground his approach to history on Qur'anic and/or sound traditional sources. Did our Prophet not warn us that Islam began as a stranger in this world and will return as a stranger?[3] Did he not expect that the Muslims will split up into 73 sects—after the Jews had split into 71 and the Christians

---

1. A. J. Wensinck, *Concordances et indices de la tradition musulmane*, 8 vols. Leiden: 1962-1992, 1,500 (. . . *wa yahlifūna wa lā istahlafūna* . . .).

2. No. 188.

3. Wensinck, *Concordance*, 4:70a.

into 72—thus frustrating Islam's progress as a whole altogether?[4] On the other hand, has God's religion not seen a revival every time that it has declined? And do we not expect a rejuvenator of Islam (*al mujaddid*) at the beginning of each century and particularly at the beginning of each millennium?[5]

Abū Ḥamīd al Ghazzālī (d. 111 C.E./505 A.H.) considered himself such a revificator, as can be deduced from the very title of his *Iḥyā' 'Ulūm al Dīn*. Ibn Taymīyah (d. 1328 C.E/728 A.H.), Shāh Wālī Allāh (1763 C.E./1176 A.H.), and Muḥammad ibn 'Abd al Wahhāb (d. 1787 C.E./1201 A.H.)—founder of the irreplaceable Wahhābī movement—as well as Muḥammad 'Abduh (1905 C.E./ 1323 A.H.), al Ustādh al Imām, may also be counted among those revivers of Islam.[6] At any rate Aḥmad-i Sirhindī (1624 C.E./1034 A.H.) even accepted the title of "renovator of the second (Muslim) millennium" (*mujaddid alf thānī*).

Our optimists might point out that it is highly doubtful whether there have ever been entirely "good times" for Islam after the lifetime of the Prophet. Has Islam really ever been fully realized during the Umayyad, 'Abbāsid, or Ottoman periods, or even in Muslim Spain? Does knowledge and wisdom not accumulate over time? Are we not in a better position today to understand certain Qur'anic *āyāt* of a scientific nature? For instance, ayah 2 of Surat al 'Alaq contains the word *'alaq,* which was assumed to mean "blood clot," is now known on the basis of medical microscopy to mean a "clinging germ-cell."[7]

---

4. It is perhaps significant that this hadith is not reported by al Bukhārī and Muslim. However, it is found in the four other *ṣaḥīḥ* compilations of Abū Dāwūd, al Tirmidhī, al Dārimī, and Ibn Hanbal.

5. Wensinch, *Concordance,* 1:324 (. . . *man yushaddidu* . . .).

6. Shaykh Muḥammad 'Abduh, *Risālat al Tawḥīd* (Cairo: 1897).

7. Maurice Bucaille, *The Bible, The Qur'an and Science*, 5th ed. (Paris: 1988), chapter 7; Maurice Bucaille, *The Qur'an and Modern Science* (Riyadh: n.d.), 16; and Mohamed Talbi et Maurice Bucaille, *Reflexions sur le Coran* (Paris: 1989), 233-34.

The optimist, he too, can fortify his views with scriptural evidence. Is he not a member of the best community that has ever been brought forth for mankind (3:110) and which can bring about positive changes in this world—provided that it changes its attitudes: morals and morale? When our Lord tells us: "Verily, Allah does not change men's condition unless they change their inner selves" (13:11), does this not mean that He *will* help us if we do indeed change our ways, not through "reforming" Islam but through reforming our attitude toward it? Will there not be a time when one will see people enter God's religion in hosts (110:2)?

Our pessimist might retort that there are two hadiths, reported independently by Jabīr ibn 'Abd Allāh and by Abū Hurayrah, according to which Allah's Apostle said: "*Behold, people have entered God's religion in hosts—and in time they will leave it in hosts*"—reading Sūrat al Naṣr not as a projection into the future but linking it with the historical events following the submission to Islam of Makkah. Such a skeptic could paraphrase quotations from Muḥammad 'Abduh and French Sufis, according to which Islam may have emigrated from the Muslim world, where one now finds many Muslims but little Islam.

CHAPTER 2

A Bit of Optimism

It may be more fruitful to look at the world as it is now than to base predictions on Muslim futurologist doctrine. And what do we see if we rub our eyes a little? Is Islam really advancing? Or is it perhaps, appearances aside, in decline? Or are the Muslims perhaps just muddling along, on the fringes of history, as they have been doing for several centuries, easy prey for physical and mental colonization? But this time, let us hear the optimist view first.

One has to read the depressing reports on life and mores in Makkah al Mukaramah and in al Madinah during the last century in order to appreciate the moral and physical progress made ever since. We have reliable descriptions given in great detail by western Makkan pilgrims like the Swiss Muslim Johann Ludwig Burckhardt. He lived in Makkah and al Madinah for six months in 1814-15.[8]

His observations were corroborated both by the wavering British Muslim Sir Richard Burton, who visited Makkah and al Madinah in 1853,[9] and the German non-Muslim, Heinrich von Maltzan, who stayed in Makkah in 1860.[10]

All three authors confirmed that the holy places of Islam at that time were in decay, filthy, insecure, and full of superstitions. Believe it or not, alcohol and prostitutes were offered right in front of the *ḥaram* and occasionally even inside, and prayer was loosely

8. Johann Ludwig Burckhardt, *In Mekka und Medina* (Berlin: 1994).

9. Richard Burton, *Personal Narrative of a Pilgrimage to Al-Madinah and Meccah*, 2 vols. (New York: 1964).

10. Heinrich von Maltzan, *Meine Wallfahrt nach Mekka* (Tübingen: 1982).

observed, even by pilgrims. In those days, their number, decreasing year by year, was only 70,000 in 1814 (Burkchardt's estimate) and already down to 30,000 in 1860 (von Maltzan's estimate).

Indeed, after Napoleon's invasion of Egypt and the successive breaking apart of the Ottoman empire in the nineteenth and early twentieth centuries, politicians and orientalists alike foresaw the complete disappearance of Islam within their lifetimes. They studied Islam as a cultural phenomenon that one should record for posterity before it vanished entirely. In this spirit, the French colonizers for instance could appreciate 'Abd al Qādir, the great Algerian hero, statesman, and Sufi, only as a quaint folkloristic figure with some nuisance value.[11] Personalities who even at that time sympathized with Islam like, for instance, Johann Wolfgang von Goethe (d. 1832) only liked its unmitigated monotheism but not Islam as lived in the Muslim world.[12]

Against this depressing background, when one performs hajj or umrah today, it is startling to realize how much has been achieved.

The Makkan *ḥaram* and the Prophet's Mosque in al Madinah have been beautifully enlarged to hold between 480,000 and 650,000 pilgrims, and yet they are too small for the ever-increasing number of believers who want to perform their obligatory pilgrimage. The number has to be limited through national quotas for visa. Alcohol has been banished, theft is barely known, single ladies are not admitted, and prayer is universally observed.

A reversal of orientalist attitudes toward Islam, observable since the early twentieth century, was a harbinger of further positive change. Rather than studying Islam like the infamous Lawrence of Arabia in the interest of British imperialism, there was now an elite group of European academics who embraced Islam wholeheartedly.

---

11. Bruno Etienne, *Abdelkader* (Paris: 1994).

12. Ahmed von Denffer, "Der Islam und Goethe," 20 installments, *Al-Islam*, (Munich) no. 1 (1990) to no. 3 (1994).

Among them were René Guénon, Martin Lings, Titus Burckhardt, and of course Leopold Weiss, alias, Muhammad Asad. And among the orientalists who refrained from formally converting to Islam, there were personalities—like Jacques Berque, Louis Massignon, Denise Masson, and Annemarie Schimmel—who were seen to be on the brink of pronouncing the *shahādah*.

Many of their orientalist colleagues, at any rate, no longer studied their subject—Islam—with disgust and barely disguised hatred but with sympathy and empathy.

Simultaneously, since the 1930s, grassroots Muslim revival movements put Islam onto the political agenda of almost every country within the *dār al Islām* region. Their common prototype remains the Egyptian Muslim Brotherhood, founded by Ḥassan al Bannā (d. 1949),[13] and their preachers, i.e., in addition to other authorities like the father of Muslim liberation theology, Sayed Quṭb (d. 1966), as well as Abūl A'lā al Mawdūdī (d. 1979), Shaykh Kishk, and Muḥammad al Ghazzālī.

But revival did not only come from below. Both the Wahhābī and Sanūsī movements, and to some extent also the Ṣalafiyah à la Muhammad 'Abduh, brought about a Muslim revival from the top, greatly expanded by the possibilities of petro-dollar financing. As it so happens, the richest persons in the world today—the Sultan of Brunei, King Fahd, and Amir Zayed of the United Arab Emirates—are all Muslims, giving important impulses to Islamic *da'wah* worldwide. Just think of the many millions of copies of the Qur'an being distributed for free, also in model English and French translations, from the King Fahd Printing Center in al Madinah.

In sum, this development, perceived as a "fundamentalist" threat both inside the Muslim region and by the world at large, turned Islam into the most topical media subject of the last quarter of this century.

---

13. *The Five Tracts of Ḥassan al-Bannā* (Berkeley and Los Angeles: 1978), are still basic material.

Islam is no longer expected to disappear but rather to expand and even to explode. NATO generals, when making operational plans, are advised to take into account that the most likely military confrontation of the future will not be an East–West but a North–South conflict, Islam being the new expansive and aggressive potential enemy.

This fear is brought home by emigrant and local Muslims, whose number is visibly increasing almost everywhere. Some five million Muslims now live in the United States and 2.5 million in Germany. The Muslim population of Great Britain is around 3 million and 3.5 million in France. The total number of Muslims in 1991 was given by western sources as 990,547,000—(conservative) numbers causing fear and trepidation.[14]

Thus mosques are now springing up all around the world, from Los Angeles and Moscow to Rome and Zagreb. In Cordoba, former seat of the Umayyad *khilāfah*, Spanish Muslims in 1994 founded the International Islamic University "Averroës" of al Andalus. Not far from the fantastic old mosque of Cordoba, a *mu'adhdhin* is again calling for prayer. What a provocation, this happening five centuries after the last Muslim had been expelled from Spanish soil!

All this is symptomatic of the fact that *Islam worldwide is the only growing religion.*

In 1934 already Muhammad Asad (d. 1992 C.E./1412 A.H.) had made startling predictions about the ascension of Islam in his famous pamphlet "Islam at the Crossroads," written in Delhi. Rather than being apologetic or imitative versus the West in the Ṣalafiyah manner, Asad described Islam as a complete and sound alternative program for life, contrasting it plainly with the decadent materialism of contemporary western civilization (which included the Soviet Union).

14. See the article "Anzahl der Muslime in der Welt," *DLM-Rundbrief* (Hamburg), (February 1991); see also *Yearbook of the Encyclopedia Britannica, 1996*, which shows that Muslims in the world constitute (1,126,525,000) one-fifth of the world population, pp. 310-311.

Asad foresaw World War II as an inevitable global struggle between the atheistic capitalist West and the equally atheistic communist East. He predicted that their antagonism would spell disaster for both of them, "leading the material self-conceit of Western civilization in such a gruesome way ad absurdum that its people will begin, once more, . . . to search after spiritual truth; *and then a successful preaching of Islam may become possible*" (my emphasis).

These visions of more than sixty years ago had seemed imprecise after World War II when the Occident, rather than collapsing, split into two superpower camps which seemed to stabilize each other for decades to come.

Today, after the bankruptcy of communist ideology and system evident since 1990 and the alarming signs of a spiritual and value crisis in the West, we know that Muhammad Asad was right after all: Christianity is going through a virtual change of paradigm, and the so-called "project of modernism" is failing under our very eyes.

Western theologians and scientists have begun to doubt whether their basic assumptions are valid after all.

Chapter 3

Christology Revisited

This spiritual crisis of the Occident can perhaps be demonstrated best through an analysis of current Christian christology, i.e., current clerical views on the role and nature of Jesus.

In this respect, too, Muhammad Asad was remarkably far-sighted when writing, also in 1934:

> Perhaps the most important intellectual factor which prevented Europe's religious regeneration was the current conception of Jesus Christ as the Son of God . . . . European thinkers instinctively shrunk back from the conception of God as presented in the teachings of the Church: and as this was the only conception to which they had been accustomed, they began to reject the very idea of God, and with it, of religion.

How right he was. As we shall see, that is exactly where we now are.

In order to understand this fully and to see the extraordinary current potential for change, we must recall the scandalous Council of Nicaea (325) and its fatal doctrinal consequences for the following sixteen centuries.

In 325, the (still) heathen Roman emperor Constantine I ("Constantine the Great")—and not Pope Sylvester I—convened an ecumenical council to the town of Nicaea (now Iznik), 195 km. by road south of Byzantium (now Istanbul). This first Council of Nicaea, opened by the emperor on 20 May 325 and attended by as few as

225, almost exclusively Eastern churchmen, was prompted by Constantine to adopt the so-called fides Nicaena (Nicene Creed), which until now determined and cemented the dogmatic split between Christians on the one hand and Jews and Muslims on the other.

Without advance written preparation or proper discussion, the prelates adopted a formula, presented by the pagan emperor, stating that *Jesus Christ as the Son of God was truly God himself, not created but engendered by God Father and "consubstantial" (homoúsis) with Him.* This laid the foundation for the dogma of divine incarnation and, in consequence, for the concept of the Trinity.

The immediate results were tragic enough because the majority of Christians at the time, followers of Bishop Arius from Alexandria as well as Christians of Jewish background, had all along maintained that Jesus was not consubstantial with God but rather a human being chosen by God—in other words, a prophet. They were now considered and persecuted as "heretics."[15]

Much time and effort have been spent since by both Catholic and Protestant theologians and philosophers trying to understand and to explain rationally the dogmas of Incarnation and Trinity. Invariably they failed—how else could it be? Consequently, they resorted to the supposedly infallible argument that both dogmas simply were mysteria.

Of course, in doing so they disregarded that not the slightest basis for the assumption of such mysteria could be found in any authentic message of Jesus. On the contrary, like Muhammad, Jesus considered himself as a purely human being.

On their part, undisturbed by Catholic doctrine, the Muslims held on to their own christology as set out with great precision and clarity in the Qur'an, according to which Jesus was:

---

15. In view of these and other circumstances, Karl Deschner gave his critique of Church history the title *Kriminalgeschichte des Christentums* (Criminal History of Christendom), 2 vols. (Reinbek: 1986-88).

- like Adam created (and not engendered) (3:47 and 59, 23:91, 112:3);
- born from a virgin (3:47);
- confirming the divine messages received before him (3:50);
- a prophet like those before him (2:136, 3:84, 6:85); and
- not one of three divine persons within a multiple deity (4:171 and 5:73).

Even so-called Muslim modernists and "cultural Muslims" never challenged this Islamic concept of Jesus.

During the last two centuries, it has also dawned on the Christian world that it is untenable indeed to say "God has taken unto Himself a son" (Qur'an 18:4–5 and 19:88–89). Indeed the glaring loss of credibility of the official dogma on Jesus largely explains the spreading of atheism and agnosticism during that period and the ever-growing rejection of the established churches by people taking refuge with esoteric faiths—from anthroposophy and feminist theology to Buddhism and Red Indian Shamanism.

Therefore, it was only natural that the last sixty years has seen bold attempts at a reinterpretation of the status of Jesus within Christian orthodoxy. The Protestant thinkers Karl Barth (d. 1968) and Rudolf Bultmann (d. 1976) and the Jesuit professor Karl Rahner were pioneers on this road.

Barth considered Jesus as a human being "only" but uniquely chosen by God for his mission—a formidable status indeed. With his historical-critical method Bultmann "demythologized" the New Testament to such an extent that most theologians today agree on the impossibility of reconstructing the historical Jesus; the New Testament simply does not provide sufficient authentic foundations for it. Rahner, in turn, engaged in intellectual acrobatics to undo the Council of Nicaea. On the one hand, he was courageous enough to reshape the incarnation theory by stating that Jesus essentially was a human being characterized by total submission to God (*Probleme der Christologie heute*). According to him, divine incarnation in the sense of inspiration was a possibility theoretically open to everybody, Jesus having been the perfect example of such divine intervention. On the other hand, the same professor Rahner formulated the blasphemy that God after all could, if He so chose, create the possibility of a co-deity . . . .

This might suffice to show that Christian christology is in deep crisis. "As it is, behold, they who have inherited the divine writ from those who preceded them are (now) in grave doubt, amounting to suspicion, about what it portends" (42:14) (trans. Muhammad Asad).

Contemporary Catholic and Protestant theologians alike are trying to keep afloat by dumping overboard, a bit belatedly, as much as possible of untenable formula of belief.

Thus within the Christian camp one can discern today the following three positions on christology:

- Jesus was not a historical person;
- Jesus was a model man, inspired and chosen by God, but not consubstantial with Him; nor did he rise from his grave;[16]
- Virtues and vices are equally spread among the followers of all religions; they all represent valid, while limited perspectives of the same reality (Paul Schwarzenau; John Hick).

The first of these positions led to the mystical construction of a *cosmological Jesus*. The former Dominican monk Matthew Fox is indeed preaching the adoption of this new paradigm as if his speculation were viable without, at its basis, *a historical Jesus*. (Fox seems to say that the idea of Jesus is so beautiful that one should invent him if/since he did not exist.)

John Hick (Birmingham) is right in pointing out that such a suprahistorical figure of Jesus is little else but another terminology for transcendental reality.

---

16. Gerd Lüdemann, *Die Auferstehung Jesu* (The Ascension of Jesus) (Göttingen: 1994).

The second of these position runs into the difficulty that a rehumanized Jesus can hardly claim a unique position with respect to other apostles and prophets. Indeed, such a Messiah, is he not the very *Jesus of the Qur'an*?

This dilemma explains why some Christian thinkers now replace the exclusive Catholic dogma *extra ecclesiam nullum salus* (no salvation outside the church)—defunct since the Second Vatican Council (1962-65)—by a new inclusive one. They now tend to teach that Jesus brought salvation to everybody. This theory turns all Muslims neatly into what Karl Rahner called "anonymous Christians" . . . . (Thanks!) There is a grain of salt even in this hypothesis: Given the dogmatic dismantling of Jesus and his mother in the Christian world, we can conclude that *today only Muslims uphold the historical veracity and elevated status of both*!

The third position mentioned above aims at nothing less than a relativist ecumenical unity of all religions for which our "post-Christian era" is seen to be ripe.[17] This is a view that has been dear to the hearts of mystics from all ages. Jalāl al Dīn Rūmī (d. 1272), the "*Mevlana*" of Konya and inspirer of the Whirling Dervishes (*mevlevi*), propagated such an all-embracing religion of universal love already in the thirteenth century. In his *Dīwān,* one can find him saying: "I am neither Christian nor Jew, and also no Parsee and no Muslim."[18] This is a feeling of cosmic unity and togetherness so well expressed by Friedrich Schiller in the very ode chosen by Ludwig van Beethoven for his Ninth Symphony: "*Seid umschlungen, Millionen!*" ("Be embraced, oh you millions!").

The perspectives of these corrective processes are breathtaking: For the first time in fourteen centuries there is a very real chance

17. John Hick, "Wahrheit und Erlösung im Christentum und in anderen Religionen," *Religionen im Gesprach*, vol. 2 (Balve: 1994): 113-27.

18. Dschelaladdin Rumi, *Aus dem Diwan*, trans. Annemarie Schimmel, (Stuttgart: 1964).

that Christian teaching will conform to the Jewish, Christian, and Qur'anic images of Jesus.

If this should happen, Islam would have fulfilled its task in this important domain, and the Christian-Jewish-Muslim trialogue could hope, for the first time, to advance not only in social aspects but dogmatically as well. Contrary to what the Catholic professor Hans Küng had been suggesting, the status of Jesus would no longer be taboo or nonnegotiable, respectively. As a result, Christians might finally be ready to accept the Qur'an as one other genuine divine revelation and Muhammad as God's medium for it.

CHAPTER 4

What Islam Is up against

Alas, we have little reason to hope that we will now see Chris-tians enter God's religion in hosts (*Sūrat al Naṣr*:2). It is more likely that the imminent collapse of the established Christian churches will increase, in our multireligious supermarkets, the demand for esoteric experiences. Alienated from these churches, many highly emancipated and individualistic former members, rather than embracing Islam, will act like the one who makes his own desires his deity (Qur'an 45:23).

In short, Islam in the United States and in Europe, despite the momentous developments within Christendom, will most likely have to face in the twenty-first century the very mixture of attitudes so typical of Makkah at the time of our Prophet: neopaganism, agnosticism, atheism, neopolytheism, and ethnocentrism (*'aṣabīyah*), namely, people who worship idols like cocaine, astronomy, Boris Becker, or Claudia Schiffer.

In my view, the battle line is no longer the one drawn between Muslims and Christians, or Christians and Jews, but the very deep global trench dividing a minority of God-believing people—Muslims in the original sense of the word—from the majority of people for whom the notion of God has increasingly become irrelevant and meaningless; people for whom reality is limited to what we can see, touch, sniff, taste, or hear; people for whom any religious belief is mere superstition, "opium for the masses" (Marx), and a sign of self-delusion revealing a lack of logic, courage, and intelligence.

In this respect, there is no basic difference between formerly communist societies, which were exposed to an active atheist policy, and western countries. In the latter, atheism was never promoted publicly, and yet, in the form of unmitigated materialism and consumerism, it became the generally practiced form of life there as well.

Indeed, it is as if Marx, Darwin, Nietzsche, and Freud—and with them the entire positivism and scientism of the nineteenth century—in a banalized form had been absorbed and inhaled by the entire occidental population.

Muslim countries, once colonized or governed by westernized local governments, to some extent traveled the same route. Most of the Turkish "intelligentsia" of Istanbul, Ankara, and Izmir, for instance, discovered within two generations of Mustafa Kemal's rejection of their religious heritage in favor of European "modernism" that their children do not have the faintest idea about Islam. They never learn to pray and cannot even recite Sūrat al Fātiḥah.

Of course, they still celebrate *şeker bayramī* (*'īd al fiṭr*) but without having fasted, much like those Christians who celebrate Christmas without being quite sure about God and/or Jesus.

This observation is not in contradiction with the fact that Europe and the United States still consider themselves "Christian." But Christendom now only means that public opinion acknowledges a debt to a pervasive liberal and "humanitarian" civilization owing as much to the Christian as to the classical Greek and Roman heritages. Baptism, church weddings, and burials are still observed in a superstitious way: It won't hurt, and perhaps it'll help somehow. . . .

Also, many people still feel sentimentally attached to the old (and not so old), mainly pagan customs surrounding the cozy Christmas season. However, even when the Catholic German Chancellor, Helmut Kohl, addresses his nation on such an occasion, God or Jesus usually are not even mentioned. Thus basic Christian conviction and practice has receded to fundamentalist sects which in vain try to revive the Church from below.

The loss of faith in God has been compensated for in the West by a boundless faith in "progress." The world is seen to become more and more "illuminated" and "rational," liberal and humanitarian. This process of modernism, typified in the American way of life, is seen as the obligatory model for reshaping the "rest" of the world.

The average occidental, no matter which level of education, can no longer perceive of an alternative to western-style life in a thoroughly laicistic (secular) world. Sooner than later, he expects, everybody will "wear jeans, eat hamburgers, drink Coca-Cola, smoke Marl-boros, watch CNN, live in Bauhaus-shaped buildings as a citizen of a parliamentary democracy and probably be a pro-forma member of some Christian Church."[19]

This notion became particularly virulent after the collapse of communism around 1990, prompting Francis Fukuyama, head of the policy planning staff of the American State Department, in 1991 to publish his article (and later his book) proclaiming "The End of History." The message of this new thinking, in terms of a western style world order, was loud and clear: Only obscure and backward countries might still fail, for some limited time, to understand the absolute superiority of the western approach with its rationalism, liberalism, individualism, tolerance, parliamentalism, and human rights. In other words: The West generally continues to expect that the American way of life will impose itself globally.

This is an all-pervasive notion. When Hans Küng demands a "global ethics," or when Wilfred Cantwell Smith calls for the development of a "global theology," they have in mind, I suppose, an ethics and theology which—like the artificial world language Esperanto—would mainly be based on European features.[20] There

---

19. Murad Wilfried Hofmann, *Islam: The Alternative* (Reading: 1993) (Arabic version Munich/Kuwait: 1993).

20. N. Ross Reat and Edmund Perry, *A World Theology* (Cambridge, UK: 1992).

can be no doubt: The Third World is facing an Occidental "righteousness triumphant"[21] that smacks of racism.[22]

If the Islamic world does not want to live in such a monoculture, it must make a monumental effort to realize, against so many odds, a twenty-first century *dār al Islām*, i.e., a theocentric—not Eurocentric—society in which God's word is law and Islamic civilization can again be brought to a flowering.

A world in which Muslims feel at home, not as citizens but as believers and members of a single ummah . . . A world where technology, practiced by genuine Muslims, looses its dehumanizing aspects . . . A world in which all praise and subservience is due to God alone—*subḥānahu wa ta'ālā*—and not to the contemporary gods of beauty, youth, power, sex, money, popularity, status, and entertainment . . . A world not determined by the requirements of the economy and of high technology—efficiency, productivity, growth, and maximization of profit—but by an overruling concern for man and his physical, emotional, and spiritual needs.

In short, if we, the Muslims, want to be left alone we must make a gigantic effort in the sense of greater jihad in order to protect our right to cultural self-determination in a world that seeks universal assimilation. This will require, as we shall see below, a further "reconstruction of Islamic thought"[23] and practice to a point where the Muslim world can withstand the tide of postmodernism on all fronts: education, communications, political science, law, economy, and technology.

In short: It requires that Muslims by name become Muslims by conviction again. In the last resort, *there is no substitute for a reconversion of the converted.*

---

21. Robert Corfe, *Righteousness Triumphant: An Approach to a Unifying World Religion* (1992).

22. Ziauddin Sardar, *Barbaric Others: A Manifest of Western Racism* (London: 1993).

23. In the footsteps but not necessarily with the approach of Muḥammad Iqbāl.

Attitudes like those professed by Mr. Fukuyama do not lend themselves to an Occidental–Oriental dialogue between equals—or to a dialogue at all. Let us be sober: Why should agnostic secularism compromise vis-à-vis the religion of Islam, since it has already managed to reduce, quite easily, the Christian religion to little more than a social service?

Why should the West be interested in reopening questions of transcendental character with Muslims after it has succeeded so splendidly in banishing such questions from its own agenda? Why should the West take the culture of Third World countries seriously when, like so many Muslim ones, the Third World has already turned itself—only too happily—into hybrid caricatures of the West?

A western tourist, finding in so-called Muslim countries wine and pork, pornography, state lotteries and government loans at 14 percent interest, the Occidental calendar and the Christian Saturday–Sunday weekend (and mostly empty mosques)—why should he take Muslim guest-workers back home seriously when they ask for *ḥalāl* meat? Will not places like Istanbul or Izmir look to him like neopagan cities inspite of the occasional (folkloristic?) call for prayer?

In the last analysis, the North–South dialogue in media exchange is already a one way street, the North having won the media game long ago. This resulted in wholesale Muslim assimilation of western ideas and approaches which now govern their lives —a plague coined "occidentosis."[24]

Given the disasters of the last century, it seems nevertheless quite incredible that occidental hubris, the naive western faith in unlimited progress, is still widespread.

Have people really failed to realize that the enlightened reign of rationalism and humanism did not prevent the two most savage world wars, fought with gas grenades, nuclear bombs, and "strategic

24. Jalal Ahmad, *"Occidentosis:" A Plague from the West* (Berkeley: 1982).

bombing" of civilians in cities like Dresden (this particular act being conceived by a British general, "Bomber-Harry," now honored in Britain by a monument)? Has the world ever seen worse crimes than those committed by Stalin in the Soviet Union against his own people and by German and other fascists against Jews in Nazi-German extermination camps? Is a strategy based on mutual deterrence with the threat of thermonuclear annihilation "rational"? Is it progress to have steered our planet to the brink of environmental disaster? I could go on but will not.

Western thinkers could have drawn one conclusion from this dilemma of modern rationalism, but only a few did: The horrific events of the last century prove that ethics cannot be based effectively on sheer rational insight or sentimental humanistic feelings. Only the submission of man to the ethical commands of God, and nothing but this, can achieve moral behavior even by the masses.

It is, of course, typical that scientific ideas become general conviction one hundred or more years after having been elaborated, and then in a popularized banalized form only. Thus, it is not surprising that the average contemporary occidental atheist or agnostic still follows, proudly, outdated philosophical ideas from the nineteenth century and ignores contradictory results of more recent scientific research. This is true, in particular, as far as contemporary micro- and macrophysics and brain research are concerned.

Many a stout academically trained "intellectual" atheist would be stunned if he found out how many of the most advanced physical, medical, and biological scientists of today, with the notable exception of British astronomer Stephen Hawking,[25] believe in the existence of a superior intelligence, a creator of the cosmos.[26]

---

25. Stephen W. Hawking, *A Brief History of Time: From the Big Bang to Black Holes* (New York: 1988).

26. Among them are such famous brain researchers as Nobel Prize winner John C. Eccles (*The Self and Its Brain: An Argument for Interactionalism*, [New York: 1977]) and French philosopher Jean Guitton (*Dieu et la science* [Paris: 1991]) in discussion with Grichka and Igor Bogdanov.

The evolution of physics into a postmodern science readmitting metaphysical reality was launched by such well-known figures as Max Planck (d. 1947), founder of the (energy) quantum theory; Albert Einstein (d. 1955), discoverer of the theory of relativity; and Werner Heisenberg (d. 1976) who, in 1927, enunciated the principle of uncertainty or indeterminacy after discovering that it is impossible to determine at the same time both the position and velocity of an electron (it could appear either as a particle or as a wave).

These German giants of modern physics and mathematics, as well as their colleagues Neils Bohr (quantum mechanics), Max Born, Arthur Eddington, and Erwin Schröder—to name but a few—played havoc with traditional concepts of matter, causality, time and space and thus reopened the door for the entry of religion into science. Richard Swinburn[27] concluded for them all the new *Probability Theory of God*: It is extremely improbable that God does not exist.

Indeed, a majority of the physicists just mentioned, as well as Carl Friedrich von Weizsäcker, turned, in philosophical terms, into post-Platonic idealists, namely, people who believe that a spiritual realm exists and that, perhaps, it alone is real."[28]

I do not want to suggest that this revolution went entirely unnoticed by the average man-in-the-street. But what he grasped was little more than the notions that "everything is relative," that all perception is subjective, and that human reasoning is capable only of determining its own limits—which are identical with the limits of sensual perception—as David Hume (*Enquiry Concerning Human Understanding*), Immanuel Kant (*Kritik der reinen Vernunft*), and Ludwig Wittgenstein (*Tractatus logico-philosophicus*) had been urging each at his time.

---

27. Richard Swinburn, *The Existence of God* (Oxford: 1979).

28. Hans-Peter Dürr, ed., *Physik und Transzendenz*, (Munich: 1986); Brigitte Falkenburg, *Teilchenmetaphysik, Zur Realitätsauffassung in Wissenschaftsphilosophie und Mikrophysik* (Mannheim: 1994).

In fact, badly understood modern physics neither lead to the intellectual humility typical of Abū al Ḥasan al Ash'arī (d. 936 C.E./ 324 A.H.) nor to the general recognition that our latest knowledge about the beginning of the universe and of life on Earth is in consonance with the cosmological passages of the Qur'an. Rather, modern man sees his skepticism, agnosticism, and individualism confirmed by the collapse of Marxism, Darwinism, and Freudianism. As philosopher Jürgen Habermas has put it: "Modern morality has become the very embodiment of the principle of subjectivity."[29]

In other words: People in a pseudoreligious way continue to believe that there is no salvation outside science (*extra scientiam nullum salus*) and still mistake outdated nineteenth-century materialism and positivism for that conclusive science.

It is equally disturbing that not enough western people are sufficiently aware of the malaise that has befallen their societies due to a growing sense of vacuity, a loss of meaning, and the absence of any higher purpose in life—an alarming spiritual deficit that turns individual existence into a desperate, senseless undertaking. Indeed, as Parvez Mansoor formulated: *Atheism is taking its toll on the western psyche.*

As if the catastrophic decline of western morals and solidarity were not obvious: Crime, alcoholism, drug addiction, publicly advertised homosexuality, child abuse, the rampant divorce rate, hard pornography, and a lack of civic spirit are symptoms of decadence. The worst of these is perhaps the trend of young women and men to live as "singles." No one can yet assess the damage done to a whole generation of youngsters growing up without a father.

This moral predicament is accompanied and reinforced by a debilitating loss of certainty. People realize that history does not

---

29. Jürgen Habermas, *Der Philosophische Diskurs der Moderne* (Frankfurt: 1985).

unfold as predicted. The fall of communism was followed by a very short period of occidental triumphalism. People soon noticed that the world, rather than entering—thanks to a "new world order"—an era of eternal peace was regressing into nineteenth-century nationalism and chauvinism that, in turn, was causing savage wars like that waged by Greek Orthodox and communist Serbs against both Croatia and Bosnia-Herzegovina and that waged by Russia against the Muslims in the Caucasus region.

People are unsettled as well when realizing that the so-called civilized world is neither capable of limiting an ever-increasing devastation of the environment fueled by an ever-increasing compulsive, if not obsessive, surplus consumption. The ensuing symptoms, like smog over large cities, provoke Doomsday visions.

But hedonism cannot be curbed. Decadence has sapped occidental will power, and ecology as a pseudoreligion simply cannot replace the normative and motivational functions of religion, nor supply a new and binding code of values.

CHAPTER 5

Islam and the West: Another Showdown?

It would not be fair to charge the current western neocolonialist approach, Euro-American cultural imperialism, with a complete lack of tolerance vis-à-vis religious manifestations. On the contrary, even the most enlightened persons might take a sociological interest in certain religious manifestations like theosophy and Buddhism.

Indeed, in Europe or the United States today, one can join a Hindu guru or practice Red Indian Shaman magic without danger to one's job or life. As long as business and the political establishment are not challenged—as by Christian Scientists—adherence to exotic religions is considered harmless and, at worst, quaint or queer. Normally, religious affiliation is treated as a private affair, like some colorful folklore. On the whole, one follows the unofficial doctrine of the Aquarian Age: Anything goes—except if the religion concerned is Islam. *In fact, Islam is the only religion that cannot count on benign neglect or sincere toleration.*

The reasons for this extraordinary state of affairs are manifold and complex. In fact, some reach far back into the bloody history of Christian–Muslim warfare and struggle for political and commercial domination in the Mediterranean region.

Historically, Christian enmity toward Islam is based on the assumption that Muhammad was an impostor. In Christian eyes it was wrong that the Jews clung to their Mosaic faith and rejected Jesus, but somehow it was understandable because of the natural tendency of people to hold on to traditional customs and beliefs. (Is not the reaction of the Jews to Jesus similar to the reaction of Abū Sufyān and his fellow Makkans to Muhammad and Islam?)

But when a new faith appeared—six centuries after Christ—the Christians (those who were locked into the dogma of the Trinity and could not conceive of a new message from God) considered it not only a provocation but an insult. Muslims should find it relatively easy to understand this reaction because they, too, consider their Prophet as the bearer of the final revelation (5:3) and as the seal (*al khātim*) set over all previously revealed scriptures: "Muhammad is . . . God's Apostle and the Seal of all Prophets" (33:40). Thus Muslim reaction to sects claiming to have received further divine guidance—like the Druzes and the Baha'i and Qadianis—resembles early Christian reaction to themselves.

A second historical reason for growing enmity was the Christian perception that Islam was a militant, aggressive religion that owed its expansion mainly to military operations. How else could one explain the incredibly quick spreading of Islam from the Hijāz to Constantinople (668), India (710), and central France (733)? The Christian world simply could not admit to itself that Islam had come as a liberator to peoples suffering under intolerant and arbitrary Caesarean and Papal rule and that the many "heterodox" Christians, outlawed by the Council of Nicaea, welcomed Islam as teaching what they had continued to believe: That Jesus had not been the Son of God. People thus deserted the churches for Islam in what can be termed a mass movement.

How else could a handful of backward Arabs have conquered empires? But to this day, in order to save face, the Christian world holds on to its self-fabricated legend that Islam was spread "by fire and the sword."[30]

---

30. Typical of this type of disinformation is Willy Dietl's *Heiliger Krieg für Allah*, (Munich: 1983).

The Christian gut reaction also resulted in the allegation that Muhammad, the "Impostor," had copied (badly) some teachings of Christ. In addition, the appeal to his creed was to be explained by its supposed sexual permissiveness. Did not Islam allow four wives, and was not the Prophet a sex maniac—later (and recently by Salman Rushdie) to be called "Mahound" (derogatory corruption of Muhammad)? Thus, *the contempt of Islam became an integral part of the European mentality*. During the eleventh through the thirteenth centuries C.E., this explosive emotional cocktail of false notions engendered the militant and intolerant "spirit of the Crusades," out of which, ultimately, modern Europe was born.

What interests us today is not the infamous nature of the Crusades as the earliest manifestation of a European imperialism that trampled upon each and every one of the high ideals and postulates of Christianity.[31] The Muslims to this day, thanks to their collective memory, do recall the horrors of the Crusades.

But this emotional heritage is less portentous for the imminent future than another after-effect of the Crusades: The *cultural shock* received by Christian knights when encountering the vastly superior civilization of the supposedly barbaric Saracens. Many a knight returned deeply disturbed by what he had seen and experienced in the Holy Land: A superbly refined standard of life unknown to contemporary Europe, literacy, medical science, chivalry, and tolerance as embodied by the Kurdish hero Ṣalāḥ al Dīn. It was a civilization similar to the one which had flourished in Muslim Andalusia, putting to shame their Christian opponents and revealing that if there were *barbarians*, it was *them.*

These experiences are at the bottom of the phenomenon of why Europeans still, and again, are *afraid* of Islam—an anxiety that culminated during the Turkish sieges of Vienna (1529 and 1683).

---

31. Amin Maalouf, *Les Croisades vues par les Arabes* (Paris: 1983).

It would be a dangerous illusion to believe that the spirit of the Crusades has disappeared. On the contrary. As late as 1463, Pope Pius II issued a Bull of Crusade directed against the Ottomans, in reaction to the fall of Constantinople to Sultan Mehmet II Fātiḥ ten years earlier.

Also the *reconquista* of Muslim Spain did not terminate with the expulsion of the entire Jewish and Muslim populations after 1492; the Spanish immediately tried to reconquer the shores of North Africa in the western Mediterranean and established bases in Algiers, Oran, Mellila, and Ceuta.

In the sixteenth century, the Portuguese tried to copy the Spanish along the Atlantic coast of Morocco. Their bases were found in Azila, Larache, El-Jadida (Marzagan), Safi, and Es-Saouira (Mogador). The young Portuguese king Sebastião in 1578 earnestly tried to re-Christianize Morocco. Losing the "Battle of the Three Kings" near Ksar el-Kebir, his crusade ended, however, in disaster—for himself and his country. The king lost his life, and Portugal lost its North African possessions to the Kingdom of Spain.[32]

The colonization of almost the entire Muslim world by Great Britain, France, Italy, the Netherlands, and Russia during the nineteenth century neatly fitted into this pattern. To re-Christianize the Berbers of the Maghrib, a special missionary order, the White Fathers (Pères Blancs et Mères Blanches) was founded in occupied Tunis. As regards the way the British disposed of Palestine during our century, did their approach differ much from the way the Crusaders established and ran their Frankish kingdoms in the area?

Against this background, it will surprise no one to learn that the Greek king Constantine, when attempting to reconquer western Anatolia in 1922, did not set foot on Turkish soil, like his army, in the harbor of Izmir (Smyrna) but nearby—where the English king

32. Jean Brignon et al., *Histoire du Maroc* (Casablanca: 1967), 196, 209-10.

Richard I (the Lionhearted) had landed during his *crusade,* the Third Crusade, in 1190. . . .

The current Serbian war against the Muslims in Bosnia-Herzegovina was hailed both by the Serbian and the Greek press as a crusade which aims at eliminating from Europe the last Muslim society on its soil.

Unbelievable but true: *Wars of religion have returned to the world stage,*[33] and Bosnia is not the last but only the most recent crusade.[34] People, all over again, ask each other "whose side God is on."[35] In fact, *the age of the Crusades never ended.*

Today, it may not be the Pope who is calling for a campaign against Muslims, but rather it may be the United Nations Security Council, calling for international intervention to "save a failed State" (Muslim of course) or to enforce an arms embargo against a Muslim state victim of aggression. Yes, if one scratches a little the surface of the European psyche one will find, under thin lacquer, anti-Islamic feelings—the trauma of Vienna—that can be instrumentalized at any time. And this is exactly what happened during the last twenty years in western Europe as well.

Due to the horrific crimes resulting from European anti-Semitism, the Jews left in Europe seem to be relatively safe from new pogroms. But what will happen when latent *racism is mobilized against the other Semites, the Arabs and other people of that Semitic, "Arabic religion"*? Already, there is hardly a day when a mosque is not attacked somewhere in Europe. Is there to be an anti-Islamic "Crystal Night,"[36] this time by installments, again carried

33. Karen Armstrong, *Holy War: The Crusades and Their Impact on Today's World* (New York: 1988).

34. Akbar S. Ahmad, "Bosnia: The Last Crusade," *The Arab Review* (London: 1993).

35. James and Mart Hefley, *Arabs, Christians and Jews: Whose Side is God on?* (Hannibal, MO: 1991).

36. The Nazis used this term to refer the demolition of Jewish property, organized by them all over Germany, on 9 November 1938.

out by people of good conscience, saving their motherlands from human cockroaches? I wish I were overstating the danger.

But let us not blame the other side alone. Unfortunately, the Muslim world has contributed much to the fostering of a negative image, soiling its own image. At any rate, the perception in the West of certain events in Iran and Libya, as well as the invasion in God's name of Kuwait by Ba'thist Iraq, have reinforced existing prejudices. Whether we like it or not, whether it is justified or not, Islam has become associated in the western mind with fanaticism, brutality, intolerance, violence, despotism, violation of human rights, and obscurantism.

Alas, it is indeed difficult to point out an existing Muslim state where Islam is practiced fully and nearly impossible to show a fully operative model of an Islamic economy that could be accepted universally . Also, there is no use denying that the Muslim world has been shying away for far too long from a constructive unapologetic discussion of human rights issues. (I will enlarge on these and other shortcomings below.)

For all these reasons, there is no denying the fact that Islam is currently seen as being squarely "at war with modernity."[37] Wilfred Cantwell Smith is therefore right when he observes that the"recent Western fear and bitterness expressed in anti-Communism were relatively mild, and strikingly short-lived, in comparison with centuries of medieval anti-Islamic perceptions and emotions."[38]

Anti-Islamic emotions currently materialize in several ways of which negligence, a double standard, and aggressive racist atheism may be the most prominent. To start with a typical example of neglect. Year after year we find new textbooks on the history of philosophy, including international bestsellers like Jostein Gaardner's

---

37. David Pryce-Jones, *At War with Modernity: Islamic Challenge to the West (*London: 1992).

38. Wilfried C. Smith, in *What is Scripture*? (London: 1993).

ingenious *Sofie's World.*[39] In virtually none of them is there a decent acknowledgment of Muslim philosophy. Ibn Sīnā' and Ibn Rushd might be mentioned, but only under their latinized names (Avicenna and Averroës) and in the context of Catholic scholasticism.

Al Kindī, al Rāzī, al Fārābī, al Ash'arī, the Mu'tazilah school, al Ghazzālī, al Suhrawārdī, Ibn al 'Arabī—usually they are all overlooked. And this in spite of the undeniable fact that the classical Greek and Hellenistic heritage of Europe, in particular the greatest part of the oeuvre of Aristotle, as of the thirteenth century, was transmitted to the Occident thanks to Muslim philosophers who safeguarded and developed Greek philosophy and science.

Part of this phenomenon is the unforgivable ignorance with respect to the admittedly near-incredible cultural achievements, from the eight to the fifteenth centuries C.E, in Muslim Andalusia.[40] To put it simply: *To be ignorant about Islam and its culture, in Europe or the United States, is not yet considered a lack of education.*

It is evident that the Occident applies two different criteria—*a double standard*—to itself (and other world regions) and to Muslim affairs. Let us take western media as a prime example. When a terrorist attack is reported from outside the Muslim world, we may hear that "militants of the IRA" or "members of the separatist ETA movement" threw a grenade—never will we hear of "a fanatic Catholic" or a "fanatic Socialist." Even the Sarin nerve-gas attack on the Tokyo metro system in March 1995 was attributed by western media only to a "radical" sect—not to a fanatical sect. If, on the other hand, a grenade is throw by someone in the Near East or in Algeria, the act is invariably attributed to "a fanatic Muslim," even if the Arab concerned was an Arab Christian or a Ba'athist atheist.

---

39. Jostein Gaardner, *Sofies verden* (Oslo: 1991).

40. Salmā al Khaḍrā' al Jayyūsī, ed. *The Legacy of Muslim Spain* (Leiden and New York: 1992); Sigrid Hunke, *Allahs Sonne über dem Abendland, Unser arabisches Erbe* (Stuttgart: 1960).

Let us take my own case. Weeks before the German version of my book *Islam: The Alternative* was printed in 1992, certain members of the German media launched a hate campaign against me, demanding that I be withdrawn as German ambassador to Morocco. Without them having read my book, I was accused of promoting polygyny, the beating and stoning of women, and the amputation of hands and feet. (Salman Rushdie's infamous book had at least been read before he was accused of blasphemy.)

The media seem to suffer from selective perception in particular when it attributes atrocities to Islam as a religion, as if Islam had more affinity to violence than any other denomination. When actions by Iraqi president Saddam Hussein are interpreted as actions of a Muslim, why do we never read that the monumental crimes in the Soviet Union were committed by Stalin the Orthodox Christian, and those in Nazi Germany by Adolf Hitler the Catholic?

As is only fair, western media leave baptism certificates out of play EXCEPT when Muslims are concerned. Their political activity is not analyzed as politically motivated but as a result of sinister religious commands and convictions. Does one really want to provoke a comparative analysis of which religion, Christianity or Islam, has drawn behind itself a larger bloody trace through history?

Currently, there is no end to discrimination. In western Europe one can find hundreds of small *masājid* in converted flats or deserted industrial buildings. But, when Muslims try to build a proper mosque, with a minaret, a legal battle ensures—be it in Lyon or Essen. All of a sudden, city fathers seem to consider a smoke stack more aesthetic than a Turkish-style minaret. One even argues that mosques simply do not fit into central European landscape. (Are they being systematically destroyed in Bosnia for that aesthetic reason?)

Muslims have to bargain for every meter height of their minaret and—what an absurdity—even to promise that no *mu'adhdhin* will ever use it so as not to disturb the peace and quiet. This attitude clashes of course with the fact that church bells can always be rung, even at early hours. Would a Muslim call to prayer perhaps be acceptable if the *mu'adhdhin*—as suggested by a Dutch caricature—instead of *Allahu akbar* called out *bim-bam bim-bam* . . ."?

If the small Jewish communities in Europe wish to slaughter animals according to their ritual, European administrations invariably accord them this privilege. If, however, the very large Muslim communities in Europe demand the same, under many a legal pretext they are invariably denied the right to produce *ḥalāl* meat.

In the scientific community, a double standard is applied as well. It has been obvious during the last decades, particularly in the United States, that even scientific research must comply with what is considered politically correct. Thus, a biologist can still ruin his career if he dares to challenge the Darwinian evolutionary theory or if he dares to focus his research on *hereditary* factors of intelligence—just as the career of a political scientist may come abruptly to an end if he dares to question basic assumptions of the strategic American alliance with Israel.

None of these politically correct people is labeled *fundamentalist* or called a "primitive obscurantist" for basing his popular (and therefore orthodox) views on mere taboo assumptions. If a Muslim scientist, however, proceeds from the assumption that certain (Qur'anic) values are of permanent validity, he will be ridiculed.

Muslims are particularly bitter and driven to cynicism when different criteria are applied discriminately in the political field. Therefore the law of nations (international law) is frequently called "blond and blue-eyed" by frustrated Arabs. This is their way of pointing out with justified disgust that *universal law is not quite as universally applied as one should assume.*

Take, for example, a military regime which frustrates the claims to power of a "fundamentalist" Christian politician who had won the elections (Haiti). In that case, the family of nations will unite against the dictator and intervene in favor of the democratically elected government. Except if elections had been won by a Muslim "fundamentalist" party (Algeria). In this case, the military junta is tolerated by the family of nations because it is perceived as the "lesser evil" (the greater evil being of course Islam, in whatever form).

Or let us take the example of a state (Iraq) that occupies a neighboring state (Kuwait) militarily and proceeds to annex it. In such a case, the United Nations, NATO, and the United States individually may intervene massively in military fashion in order to reestablish the territorial integrity of the occupied state. The recognition of its borders will be enforced through rigorously applied international sanctions—*except* if the occupied county, be it Palestine or Bosnia-Herzegovina, is Muslim and without oil.

Does anybody still doubt that the Serbian aggression against Bosnia-Herzegovina and their revolting crime of "ethnic cleansing" would have been crushed militarily by the United States and European powers if the Serbs had been Muslims? Is it conceivable that a Christian Bosnia would have been punished by an arms embargo if it were attacked by Muslims?

Or take the *nonpermanent* Turkish invasion into northern Iraq, in March 1995, in order to fight bases maintained there by the separatist communist Kurdish Workers Party (PKK). Since Iraq, prevented by the United Nations from exercising any of its authority there, was unable to prevent PKK attacks from its territory against Turkey, this military intervention was justified under international law and even constitutes a "NATO-case." But it was, of course, criticized heavily by people who would never think of criticizing the *permanent* Israeli occupation of southern Lebanon, motivated similarly. But then, Turkey is considered a Muslim country.

The European phobia against possible Islamic states is frequently based on the assumption that such states would be incompatible with the European ideal of laicism (secularism). This assessment is of course insincere in as much as laicism is nowhere practiced in the West, except perhaps in France, as was so well observed by al Ṭahṭāwī from 1825 to 1831.[41] All the other western countries are *Christian* democracies and republics, and that by law.

In Germany, for example, God figures in the constitution (basic law). Christian holidays are observed, and Sunday is the official day of rest. The chancellor and the president of the republic address the population at Christmas. Christian religion is taught in state schools by publicly salaried teachers. Newly recruited soldiers are invited to swear an oath to God about their allegiance to the republic and its defense. The financial administration, together with the income tax, collects a "church tax" for the upkeep of officially recognized religious communities, i.e., the Catholic, Lutheran, and Reformed churches as well as the Jewish religious community. Churches enjoy the right to ring their church bells, and blasphemy is a crime figuring in the penal code. During election campaigns, Catholic bishops, at times, make disguised recommendations as to which party to shun.

In other European countries and the United States, the situation is similar. In France, laicism is handled as a pseudoreligion. *This* kind of "laicism" a Muslim state can accept. A Muslim democratic republic, in *that* sense, would also be "secular": it, too, would separate the three powers *organically* while relating them to one another *dynamically.*[42] *Therefore, it is sheer hypocrisy to reject an Islamic state on the basis of it not being "laicistic" or "secular."*

The long-term consequences of such double standards policies is tragic. Already one can sense that many young Arabs are convinced that the democratic West is not really interested in democracy with-

41. Rifā'ah al Ṭahṭāwī, *Takhlīṣ al Ibrīz fi talkhīṣ Bārīz* (Cairo: 1833).

42. Ahmida an Naifar (b. 1942), "Al Islāmiyūn," *Majallah 15-21*, no. 7, (Tunisia: 1984).

in the Arab world because of the danger that it might produce "fundamentalist" Islamic governments.

It is in line with this attitude that former convicted "terrorists" like Menachim Begin or Nelson Mandela will be fully accepted later on as democratic politicians of high stature, *except* if such former "terrorists" are Muslims or even, like 'Abbāsī Madanī, a "fundamentalist" Muslim only. Such people will hardly ever be given the benefit of doubt as far as their democratic potential is concerned.

Just as the label "fundamentalist," with its sinister connotations, will never be attached to phenomena like the Catholic Opus Dei organization, the reactionary movement of the late French Archbishop Lefèbvre, the Israeli integrists (Lubavitchers and others) and followers of Mair Kahane in New York, Catholic and Protestant terrorists in Northern Ireland, or to militant Catholic liberation theologists in South America. No, *the derogative label of "fundamentalist" is reserved for the debasement of Muslims alone*.

Even more dangerous is the conclusion drawn by many in the Islamic world from western nonreaction to massacres in Bosnia: that *Europeans would rather bear with the physical elimination of a Muslim population than tolerate a Muslim state on European soil.*

Let us not fool ourselves: Western prejudice against and defamation of Islam is such that discrimination, fear, and superiority complex can degenerate into anti-Muslim violence any day—as it did on 18 March 1995, for example, when Molotov cocktails were thrown into the Mosque and Islamic Center of Munich, Germany.

CHAPTER 6

How to Avoid Catastrophe and Serve Islam

From the previous chapters, it is obvious that the western world and Islam—North and South of the Mediterranean—are heading for a violent conflict with potentially tragic consequences for both sides, most particularly for the Muslim communities in the United States and Europe. It is high time indeed to ask what can be done, *on both sides*, about that threatening situation and to act accordingly.

Al ḥamdu lillāh, there are some sensitive people in the Occident who have grasped how critical the situation already is and who have urged redemptive measures ever since the first deadly attacks against Turkish workers' families by neo-Nazi youths in Germany. There are now a number of grassroots "civic initiatives" (*Bürger-Initiativen*) working for the reconciliation between Germans and guest-workers and students from Third World countries. Of course, Third Worldism—that romantic infatuation with exotic parts of the world—will only carry so far, but we should be appreciative of any effort to stem the new tide of national or cultural chauvinism.

Also, the Pope and high clergy of the Protestant churches now make a point of addressing the Muslim community every year at the end of Ramadan with friendly messages, and the Muslims frequently reciprocate with invitations to their mosques.

When the Munich Islamic Center celebrated its twenty-fifth anniversary in July 1993, a high-ranking Protestant pastor remarked during his address that he felt very much at home among Muslims, because with them one could talk about God without embarrassment, something no longer necessarily true in a Protestant milieu.

But building solid bridges between the North and the Islamic South requires more substantial efforts in order to demolish the ingrained prejudices against Islam. This effort should start at the grammar school level. The Iranian professor Abdoldjavad Falaturi (Islamic Scientific Academy, Hamburg), together with his German colleague Udo Tworuschka, has made magnificent progress. They analyzed the passages on Islam in hundreds of German textbooks on Catholic and Protestant religion, history, and geography, identified gross distortions,[43] and recommended correct wording for their replacement.[44] They did the same for schoolbooks in other European countries like Denmark, Finland, the Netherlands, and Italy.

The encounters between Christian and Muslim intellectuals organized in Cordoba by Roger Garaudy and supported warmly by such personalities as Professor Hans Küng serve the same purpose. But such dialogue is almost irrelevant for the scene at large.

Muslims must make a major effort to help defuse the explosive situation. I will point out several areas in which this can be done. But let me make clear from the outset that I do not call for any concessions which would touch the essentials of the Islamic faith, the Qur'an—God's own word—and the authentic Sunnah of the Prophet. The aim is not to adapt Islam to modern requirements but to revive it in such a way that its relevance for the modern age can be recognized by even the most recalcitrant Occidental.

The beauty of this endeavor is that it will serve peace while simultaneously maximizing the chances of Islam to become the number one world religion of the twenty-first century.

---

43. Abdoldjavad Falaturi et al., *Analyse der Katholischen Religionsbücher zum Thema Islam* (Braunschweig: 1988).

44. Abdoldjavad Falaturi and Udo Tworuschka, *Der Islam in Unterricht* (Braunschweig: 1991).

I submit that reforms are due on the Muslim side in at least the following fields:

- education and technology,
- women's emancipation,
- human rights,
- theory of state and economy,
- magic and superstitious practices, and
- communications.

These reforms presuppose a neater distinction between:

- Islam as religion and Islam as civilization,
- sound and fabricated *aḥādīth,*
- Shariah and *fiqh,* and
- Qur'an and Sunnah.

I am giving education and technology prominence. Everybody knows that the ummah is badly in need of reforms in these fields in order to salvage itself from subservience to foreign powers and foreign cultures.[45] *Our future will be made in these fields.*

At one time, Muslim countries had achieved a high degree of literacy. But today, analphabetism is most widely found in the Islamic world. For a People of the Book whose revelation began with the appeal: "Read!" (*Iqra'*!), this is a secular scandal. Worse, it is un-Islamic. I suspect that this situation is not entirely unconnected with the notion that fostered *taqlīd:* That it suffices to know what the Qur'an and Sunnah have taught us—as if our Prophet had not urged us to seek knowledge and wisdom wherever it could be found.

Related to such thinking is the wonderful, still vivid tradition of memorizing the entire Qur'an. Thanks to this practice, Islam was able to survive intact years of brutal suppression, such as in Albania, Red China, the former Soviet Union, and Catholic Spain.

45. 'AbdulḤamīd AbūSulaymān, *Crisis in the Muslim Mind* (Herndon, VA: International Institute of Islamic Thought, 1993).

But, like all things, memorizing texts also has its drawbacks. Even today, children all over the Muslim world still tend to learn their lessons—not only holy texts—by heart. This is, of course, an uncritical attitude. In order to make learning successful, teachers must reduce their students' overreliance on authority. Teachers must dismantle, rather than foster, their own authority and cultivate skepticism among their students. *Skepticism is the mother of all sciences.* No research or technological progress without a critical approach to "given" facts! No more premia, therefore, for voluminous doctoral theses which, at closer look, turn out to be mere compilations of previous publications without one single original thought![46]

This appeal should also be heeded by the *khaṭīb* when delivering his *khutbah* on Friday. My own impression is that those sermons, too, rarely appeal to the rational side of man and much more often to his emotions. At times I feel as if the imam is calling the faithful to an imminent battle for life or death rather than expounding a point of ethics or doctrine. Preachers in mosques should stop shouting at their audiences as if they were children. As psychologists and professors of rhetoric know so well, the higher the pitch and the louder the voice, the less credible the message. The Qur'an addresses itself to "people who think"; ulama should do the same.

Islamic ulama are usually described as not forming a clergy in the western sense. I beg to differ. In the Islamic world, the ulama also developed into an association, administering near-secret knowledge: The sheer endless body of *aḥādīth*. It is true, in theory, that every believer has access to this vast body of traditions, but, in reality, only the ulama have the time and training to cope with the cannons of the Sunnah. This, perhaps, explains the interest of certain ulama to give the Sunnah and the Qur'an equal status or—what a deviation!—to let Qur'anic *āyāt* even be "derogated" by their reading of the Sunnah.

---

46. I like to call this the "*qālā . . . qālā . . . qālā . . .* syndrome."

Islamic learning has always been vast in the field of *ādāb* (literature), and still is today. All sciences necessary for the understanding and interpretation of the Qur'an enjoy high social status—Arabic grammar, poetry, and literature above anything else. The drawback of this attitude is that the natural sciences, so much in demand today, carry lesser social prestige than *ādāb*. This was not so during the 'Abbāsid and (Andalusian) Umayyad periods. At that time, nobody was considered highly learned if he did not master medicine, mathematics, chemistry, botany, and some astronomy. *Today, one knows that one is in a Muslim country when the water toilet is not functioning . . . .*

In some Muslim quarters, one can even detect traces of technophobia. For example, Maryam Jameelah provides a theory for this by pointing out that technology is not neutral (this is correct) and therefore maintains that "there is no difference between modernization and westernization. So they cannot be separated. Since the essence of modernity is materialism, to the total exclusion of the Unseen, it is amazing how it can be presented as compatible with Islam."[47]

As I write this little pro-Islam book on an Apple Macintosh Laptop Computer, I beg to differ. The Islamic world in Andalusia was a technological world. When it passed into western hands—for instance, the windmill—did it change its quality? The Qur'anic appeal to use our faculty of reasoning is an appeal to develop natural science as well. Nor do I believe that one can outwardly baptize or Islamize technology. It will not be damaging if used by real, sincere, devout Muslims.

If we do not dare to touch so-called western technology, how could we dare expose our children to religious education in a pluralistic world? No, we cannot—and must not—go into hiding. With Jamil Qureshi, I trust that where the five pillars have a reliable foun-

47. Maryam Jameelah, *Muslim World Book Review* 6, no. 3 (Leicester 1986).

dation in the hearts and everyday lives of Muslims, Islamic sensitivity will secure such an aversion that it will give immunity to the bits and pieces of western culture that are antithetical to Islam?. If this were not so, as in the Broadway musical, we should "stop the world and try to get off" or resign to see the Muslim world being turned into a natural park.

Nowadays, the Islamic world can even be put to shame by the highly specialized knowledge on things Islamic acquired by western orientalists—personalities like Henri Laoust, Bernard Lewis, Daniel Gimaret, or Tilman Nagel, to name but a few. Ahmad Deedat aside, *where are the qualified Muslim "occidentalists" so necessary for a North-South dialogue*?

In the field of education and science, there is, of course an ongoing reform effort to bring about an "Islamization of knowledge." Alas, I consider some of this work as misguided, inasmuch as true science is without ideological coloring. I know that in actual life science is frequently subject to ideologically colored hypotheses. But this does not mean that Muslims should try to follow suit. During my childhood in Nazi Germany, I was exposed to similar efforts. Ideologists tried to mark off "Jewish mathematics" from "Aryan mathematics" . . . Absurd.

My guess is that there is only one (but simple) way to Islamize knowledge—forming true Muslim scientists!

No other factor is harming the chances of Islamic da'wah as much as the occidental assessment that women in Islam are second-class citizens, marginalized, suppressed, and mummified.

The trouble is that this assessment is not without foundation, because Muslim women in many parts of *dār al Islām* are still deprived of their Qur'anic rights and status. In other words: *Many Muslim women are still living much as they did during the Jāhilīyah. It is, therefore, from these Jāhilīyah practices that they must be emancipated.*

Since the frightful institution of the harem virtually disappeared, polygyny is less of a problem for Islamic *da'wah* than the brutal African custom of female circumcision (wrongly attributed to Islam), the idea of male superiority, and the veiling of women outside the Orient.

Against this background, most Europeans and Americans still have to be convinced that women in Islam enjoy the same religious status—same rights, duties, and finality—as men: same dignity, same spirituality, same essential human nature. It is vital—and possible—to contradict the misconceptions concerning women in Islam. Otherwise, Islamic *da'wah* in the West is almost hopeless.

It is indeed easy to point out that Sūrat al Mā'idah:5 in combination with Surat al Nisa':129 should have prevented polygyny from ever becoming a Muslim custom. It will be more difficult, and for some time still quite impossible, to convince western people of the soundness of the fundamental Islamic viewpoint, according to which *men and women are called upon to play different roles (of equal dignity) in as much as they are not identical but complementary, both physically and (therefore) psychologically*. We will have to live with the fact that this attitude is anathematized by feminists all over the world and wait until nature imposes itself again.

The situation is different as far as the ignoble notion of genetic male superiority is concerned because, in spite of Sūrat al Nisā' :34, it has no valid Qur'anic basis, even though the phrase *al rijāl qawwāmūna 'alā al nisā'* for centuries was understood as meaning that men have been placed above women.

Most translations of the Qur'an into western languages, in full accordance with Muslim tradition, reveal this reading (and the macho state of mind responsible for it). Thus, according to M. Savary,[48] Lazarus Goldschmidt,[49] Max Henning,[50] Pesle and Tijani,[51] and Rudi

48. M. Savary, *Le Koran* (Paris: 1893).

49. Lazarus Goldschmidt, *Der Koran* (Berlin: 1920).

50. Max Henning, *Der Koran*, rev. Annemarie Schimmel (Stuttgart: 1962).

51. O. Pesle and Ahmed Tijani, *Le Coran*, 3d ed. (Paris: 1954).

Paret,[52] men are "superior" to, or "placed higher" than, women. Muhammad Hamidullah[53] views men as "directors of women"; Hamza Boubakeur,[54] Denise Masson,[55] and the Saudi committee on Qur'an translation[56] make us read that "men have authority over women." Sadok Mazigh[57] gives men the right to "supervise" women (*droit de regard*). All these translations reflect neatly Muslim practice. In many regions of the so-called *dār al Islām,* half of the entire population— meaning women—is prevented systematically from developing fully its human potential.

But Sūrat al Nisā':34 need not be understood that way. It may well be understood to mean that "men shall take full care of women" (Muhammad Asad[58]), that "men are the ones who should support women" (T. B. Irving[59]), or that "men are the protectors and maintainers of women" (A. Yūsuf 'Alī[60]). This is the sense given to it by Jacques Berque ("Les hommes assumes les femmes")[61] and Adel Khoury.[62]

The German language is particularly apt to render the true sense of *qawwāmūna,* if one translates it not as ***vorstehen***[63] but as

---

52. Rudi Paret, *Der Koran* (Stuttgart: 1979).

53. Muhammad Hamidullah, *Le Saint Coran* 13th ed. (Brentwood, MD: 1985.)

54. Hamza Boubakeur, *Le Coran,* vol. 1 (Paris: 1972).

55. Denise Masson and Sobhi El-Saleh, *Essai d'interprétation du Coran inimitable* (Beirut: 1985).

56. *Le Saint Coran et la traduction en langue française du sense de ses versets* (Madinah: n.d.)

57. Sadok Mazigh, *Le Coran* (Paris: 1985).

58. Muḥammad Asad, *The Message of the Qur'an* (Gibraltar: 1980); also see Fathi Osman, *Muslim Women* (Los Angeles: n.d.), 47-48.

59. T. B. Irving. *The Qur'an* (Brattleboro, VT: 1985).

60. A. Yūsuf 'Alī, *The Holy Qur'an,* 7th ed. (Brentwood, MD: 1983).

61. Jacques Berque, *Le Coran* (Paris: 1990).

62. Adel T. Khoury, *Der Koran* (Gütersloh: 1987).

63. This is the translation given by M. Ahmad Rassoul, *Al-Qur'an al-Karim und seine ungefähre Bedeutung in deutscher Sprache,* 4th ed. (Köln: 1991).

einstehen. In both cases, men are seen to step in front of women—in the case of ***vorstehen*** in order to exercise authority, and in the case of ***einstehen*** in order to protect. The implication is that *men are called upon to protect women if and as long as they need and desire protection.*

It seems to me that the role this particular Qur'anic verse has played is an *example of the adaptation of the Qur'an to existing pre-Islamic attitudes.* It is high time to go the other way and to adapt male behavior to the requirements of the Qur'an.

The situation is not dissimilar as far as the question of *ḥijāb* is concerned. The fact—often overlooked—is that it was ordered, and for good reasons, solely for the Mothers of the Faithful (Qur'an 33:53). All women are, however, admonished to draw their outer garments (*min jalābibihinna*) over their bosoms for the purpose of being seen as decent women and in order not to provoke sexually (Qur'an 33:59). This should be read in conjunction with Qur'an 24:1, which tells women not to display their charms beyond what may (decently) be apparent thereof (*illā mā ẓahara minhā*).

Traditionally, this has been interpreted as allowing only a woman's face, hands, and feet to be uncovered—and even less than that in regions where their faces are fully veiled, as in southern Algeria (M'Zab) and, until recently, in Saudi cities. According to Muhammad Asad, *illā mā ẓahara minhā* can, however, be understood as a wise clause "meant to allow for all the time-bound changes that are necessary for man's moral and social growth."[64] He points out what should have been obvious all along: "the injunction to cover the bosom by means of a *khimār* does not necessarily relate to the use of a *khimār* as such but is, rather, meant to make it clear that a woman's breasts are not included in the concept of 'what may decently be apparent' of her body and should not, therefore, be displayed."[65]

---

64. Muḥammad Asad, *The Message of the Qur'an*, 24:31, note 37.
65. Ibid., 24:31, note 38.

What Asad and others are saying may not conform with Muslim tradition in hot countries, where women have always covered their hair to protect themselves against heat, wind, and dust. This is undisputed. However, can such tradition—even if it goes back to ʻUmar ibn al Khaṭṭāb, disallow a freedom in principle granted to women by God?

Today, in all northern countries, the sight of a woman's hair is not considered sexually provocative. No women is taken as a whore or as cheap game simply for not wearing a head scarf. In such a civilization, imposing head scarves on Muslim women is not necessary as a means of protection. It mainly serves the purpose of demonstrating that Muslim women are Muslim women. (And that may be provocative in its own way.)

Any Muslim woman should, therefore, have the right to decide for herself what is proper for her under the circumstances in which she was raised and under the circumstances in which she now lives. No matter how she decides, there may be good Islamic reasons for it. Therefore, nobody should judge her religion by whether or not she "covers" herself, or—worse—impose veiling by force. The command *lā ikrāh fī al dīn* (there is no compulsion in religion) knows of no exception.

I understand very well why Muslim jurists shied away so long from a discussion of *human* rights, as if this subject might go away by itself—rather than becoming more and more prominent in international relations. Of course, the concept of "human rights" does not appear either in the Qur'an or in compilations of traditional Islamic jurisprudence. Treatises of *fiqh* were not organized according to legal rules of higher or lower status. Indeed, the Shariʻah still cannot be taught on the basis of a legal hierarchy of norms.

As a consequence, human rights charters can now be used as a weapon against the Muslim world.[66] Indeed, "human rights talk is

66. Anouar Hatem, *L'Islam et les Droits de l'Homme* (Association Suisse-Arabe: 1974), 15.

power talk."[67] Nothing weighs as heavily on Muslim credibility as their absence from the human rights discourse, for it implies that we let others decide for us what is to be moral and immoral. What a perfect example for showing what harm a lack of creative thinking on the part of Muslim intellectuals can do to Islam.

While "human rights" as such figure neither in the Bible nor in the Qur'an, it would have been relatively easy to prove that *all classical human rights had been protected by the Qur'an one thousand years before any western effort in this direction*—not in the form of "natural rights" of the individual, but rather as a reflex in his favor of divine commands to honor and protect body and life, personal freedom, intimacy and honor, private property, etc.[68]

True, the idea of *rights* derived from nature or agreed upon by consensus is alien to Islam. For Muslims, protection of the individual's liberties and freedoms results from the correct application of duties contained in the Shari'ah. But, what matters for the intercultural dialogue is the practical result and not the theory behind it. *Islam can, therefore, be presented as a comprehensive human rights system that is complementary to the western one.*

But this happened too little and too late.[69] Thus, the world now believes that the protection of the individual's essential rights is due to developments from the English Magna Charta libertatum (1215), the Habeas Corpus Act (1679), and the Bill of Rights (1689). Indeed, these documents contributed a great deal to the formulation of human rights in the American Declaration of Independence (1776) and the French Déclaration des Droits de l'homme et du citoyen (1789).

---

67. Parvez Mansoor, "Human Rights: Secular Transcendence or Cultural Imperialism," *Muslim World Book Review* 15, no. 1 (Leicester: 1994).

68. Abūl A'lā Mawdūdī, *Human Rights in Islam*, 2d ed. (Leicester: 1980), 17-34.

69. See the "Human Rights Declaration" adopted by the OIC on 5 August 1990 in Cairo and the "Declaration of Human Rights" adopted on 19 September 1981 in London by the Islamic Council of Europe, a suborganization of the OIC.

Given these texts, the United Nations Human Rights Declaration (1948) and the two International Pacts of 1966, the Occident is now given the entire credit for the theoretical protection of human rights. (In practice, as we all know, the documents mentioned had very little effect on the actual policies of despotic states.)

Muslims must not join in the fashion of developing ever new and ever more curious "human rights," like the "right to be afraid" or the "right to ecstasy" (i.e., to drug oneself). But, the Muslim legal profession must at least begin to add chapters on the issue of human rights to their textbooks. As a minimum, we must underline that individuals are better protected, at least in principle, by divinely decreed behavior than by legal norms elaborated by parliaments. A Qur'anic injunction is not at the disposition of law makers and cannot be disposed of, even by consensus.

Better than that: We are in a position to prove that the various Muslim declarations on human rights from the western viewpoint cover almost all issues in a satisfactory manner; except two:

First, the Shari'ah makes a difference between Muslims and non-Muslims in the fields of inheritance and marriage. This inevitably results from the concept that a Muslim, as a member of the Islamic ummah, so to speak, is a "Muslim national," for his religion confers upon him a quasi-citizenship. Therefore, if a Muslim abandons his religion, this cannot but have legal consequences—just as it is when someone in the West changes his nationality. Western thinking disapproves, of course, of any rights, or loss of rights, that might flow from the adherence to a particular religion.

Second, Muslim law cannot fully follow the western fiction that there are no relevant differences whatsoever between men and women as far as their family obligations are concerned. Nor can it positively endorse homosexuality.

This latter difference between the Occidental and Oriental outlook is symptomatic of a virtual cultural clash. The Orient believes that a woman lives counter to her very nature if she seeks to imitate a man. In the Occident, feminists still believe that a woman is not fully emancipated unless she is able to imitate a man in any field. I say "still," because some of the most "liberated" American women are beginning to have their doubts about having sacrificed family, or even motherhood, to a vain career.

For the community of Muslim states, a tactical question remains open to debate: Should those that have not yet ratified the western human rights pacts do so with proper reservations, or should they rather offensively propagate their own Islamic declarations of human rights, even if this might lead to a particular zone of human rights legislation?

Whatever emerges, for goodness sake: Stop acting apologetically or as if Islam in this field has something to hide!

The Muslim posture regarding state and economy is equally dismal. It is often misunderstood but true: In spite of the fact that Muhammad founded a confederate state at al Madinah in 622,[70] Muslims still find it difficult to explain how a truly Islamic state, at the end of the twentieth century, should look.[71] Some, like Albert Hourani, believe that t his difficulty arose exactly because Islam was born in the full light of history.

Others suspect that Muslims are ill at ease with the very concept of statehood because, given the ideal of the Islamic ummah, national states are not authentic to Islamic tradition[72] but, as Vatikiotis put it, "an enduring contradiction."[73] In their view it "is politics what men do when metaphysics fails."[74]

---

70. M. Hamidullah, *The First Written Constitution in the World*, 3d ed. (Lahore: 1975).

71. No such difficulty for Muḥammad Asad. See his very learned and wise input *The Principles of State and Government in Islam*, 2d ed. (Gibraltar: 1980).

72. M. Ghayasuddin, *The Impact of Nationalism on the Islamic World* (London: 1986).

73. P. J. Vatikiotis, *Islam and the State* (London, New York, Sydney: 1987).

74. Benjamin Barber, *The Conquest of Politics* (Princeton: 1988).

Muslims, to be sure, like Marxist communists, must hope for the eventual disappearance of national states in favor of the one and only Muslim community.

The true reason for the situation described, in my view, is the enormous flexibility—divine mercy, that is—preserved in this field by the Qur'an and the Sunnah. There simply are very, very few Qur'anic ordinances, and no clear-cut Sunnah either, concerning government. This flexibility was a blessing because it saved the ummah from legal and social rigidity.

As it is, the Qur'an and the Sunnah do not prescribe, once and for all, any specific form of state or method of election. They allow for monarchies or for liberal theocracies—but also for democracies—for whatever circumstances are right and ripe. Indeed, every generation is called upon to determine for itself which form of state will suit it best.

This being said, we do have to admit that there is a terminological problem similar to the one encountered by Muslim scholars in the human rights context: The Qur'an, the Sunnah, and traditional Islamic law could not employ, of course, such key terms of modern political science as the "separation of power," "parliamentary democracy," "general elections," "republic," "checks and balances," "revolution," "party system," "sovereignty," and so on.

This does not mean, however, that Islamic doctrine after Ibn Taymīyah had nothing to offer in this respect, as a little effort of ijtihad will prove.

It is often overlooked that the Qur'an has not only decreed *government by consent and council*[75] in Surat Āl 'Imrān:159. Furthermore, Sūrat al Shūrā:37-39 makes it clear that to rule in consultation is a *major religious obligation*. Indeed, it is listed together with "pillars" of the faith, such as prayer, zakat, military defense, generosity, and abstaining from sin.

---

75. Abūl A'lā Mawdūdī, *Human Rights in Islam*, 20.

Thus, the Qur'an gives the principle of government by consultation a higher status than the institution of executive government (see 2:30; 4:59). More important yet, God made it quite clear that *the entire Muslim population is called upon to act as His vicegerent on Earth.* When Qur'an 2:30 speaks of one who is to inherit the earth, reference is made to all of mankind and not just to a head of government.

Also, in Qur'an 6:165, 27:62, and 35:39, all human beings are spoken of as *khalā'if fī al arḍ.* The same conclusion can be drawn from Qur'an 24:55. In a Muslim state, the best community that has ever been brought forth for mankind, enjoining the doing of what is right and forbidding the doing of what is wrong (Qur'an 3:110), refers to all citizens—provided that they are sincere believers.

It must be concluded from this dominant status of the ummah, and from the fundamental obligation of *shūrā,* that *consultation is not only advisory but binding in nature.* On this basis, and in view of Qur'an 3:159, there can be no doubt that a *democracy in the form of a representative (parliamentary) republic is compatible with Islam.* Whether such a republic is the ideal or the most suitable form of state in a particular case depends, however, entirely on the level of general development. A new Muslim state founded in the West would, at any rate, be conceivable only in the form of a democratic republic.

Even while Parvez Mansoor maintains that Islam has "no church, no Party and no Pontiff,"[76] a Muslim democracy must, of course, allow for an opposition (party) to dissent on individual issues—as long as it is committed to the common cause and accepts the outcome of a vote. This principle can be deduced from Qur'an 24:62 as well as from the hadith that the *differences of opinion among the learned within the Muslim community in matters of ijtihad are part of the facilitation of the Islamic Shari'ah.*

---

76. Parvez Mansoor, *Muslim World Book Review* 13, no. 1 (Leicester: 1992).

Qur'an 6:116 reminds us, however, that even majority decisions cannot guarantee a sound course of action and should therefore not be heeded in questions of religious doctrine. Western state constitutions as well do not submit all issues—for instance, human rights—to majority rule.

A Muslim parliamentary democracy will neither be a theocratic nor a secular, but rather an ideological state, with the Qur'an as its supreme law. That, too, is nothing peculiar. I do not know of any state that functions without some official or unofficial ideology—even if it be the deceptive ideology of supposed nonideology. At any rate, virtually all non-Muslim states also honor some supreme statute, which, at least in part, is not subject to possible revision.

Finally, one can deduct by implication that the Qur'an's insistence on a just government requires an independent judiciary (*'aqḍīyah*) (Qur'an 4:58, 5:8, and 57:25) within any form of state.[77] Given human nature, how could the administration of justice be better guaranteed?

Sum total: When challenged on questions of democracy, republicanism, or the separation of power, Muslims should not go into hiding or fumble around. Rather, they should assure their challengers that none of these concepts is, by nature, foreign or inimical to Islam.

Substantial inputs by Muslim political scientists do not abound, while there is no scarcity of scientific contributions by Muslim *economists*.[78] I suppose that it is a somewhat risky undertaking in many a Muslim country to discuss issues of democracy in a concrete manner. To do so with respect to economy, however, is seen as being so utopian that it may be tolerated more easily.

---

77. See the "Book of *'Aqḍīyah*" (16) in the *Ṣaḥīḥ* of Muslim.

78. In regards to this issue, the Arab-English "Review of Islamic Economics," *Journal of the International Association for Islamic Economics*, appearing in the Markfield Dawah Centre of the Islamic Foundation in Leicester, UK, should be sufficient proof in and by itself.

Why should Islamic economic science be utopian? Again, the "fault" lies with the great flexibility wisely provided for by the absence of rigid norms in the Qur'an—with the notable exception of *ribā* (interest). The *āyāt al ribā* (verses of interest), however, helped blow the issue out of proportion. Worse, given the practice of keeping enormous interest-earning petrodollar accounts, the injunction against *ribā* has made Muslims look like a bunch of hypocrites.

We should squarely admit that an *Islamic economy will never be—cannot be and does not want to be—as efficient or as profitable as the western economy*, which treats people as economic animals. If we were to imitate the economic approach of the West, we would have to submit each and every aspect of life to the requirements of industrial production. As in the Occident, all aspects of life would be ruled by the laws of economy, and we would all strive for the maximization of profit, optimization of production, and the utter limitation of costs.

In the process, the Islamic world would become as materialistic as western society and would also lose its major advantage: The Oriental quality of life resulting from the fact that God and man, and not economy or technology, are at the center of concern. This is the very difference between a society ignoring *al ākhirah* (the afterlife) and a society of transcendental orientation. Syed Nawab Haider Naqvi is therefore right when he sums it all up in the terse phrase: "Islam negates the capitalist mentality."[79]

So let us tell them without qualms: *Muslims do not want to adapt to the western pattern of economics*. Period.

Also, the discussion of *ribā* frequently has been misdirected. Interest on capital has several key functions in a western economy, such as the large accumulation and efficient allocation of capital, efficiency control, an anticyclical financial policy, and the defense of currency exchange rates.

79. S. H. N. Naqvi, *Ethics and Economics* (Leicester: 1981), 19.

This central importance of interest on capital implies, however, that abolishing *ribā* is not a magic wand with which to transform a traditional economy—as if this could be done by a trick. Capital cannot be "Islamized" just by abolishing *ribā*.[80] On the contrary, the abolishment of interest is only feasible within an economy that is already Islamic, thanks to sincere Muslims acting as Muslims in it.

This being said, there should be much room for true ijtihad designed to determine what the message of *ayāt al ribā* is today. During the Prophet's time, interest payments were extremely excessive and consumer credit was often given to assure the survival of the poorest, a process that lent itself to exploitation. Also, in a hard currency trade economy without much technological accumulation, there was neither the demand for large capital accumulation nor the need to off-set inflationary losses.[81]

Such an analysis, at a minimum, should let us read *ribā* today as "usury" and not simply as "interest."

It seems to me to be more important to maintain the essence of Qur'an 2:275-79, 3:130, and 30:39: The overriding principle of risk sharing. This principle might not be involved in the case of small savings accounts maintained with large banks, or when fully insured cars are bought with credited installment payments. But the sharing of risks—sharing profits and losses—must become the guiding principle in all large business enterprises. In demanding this, Islam can remind western businessmen of their former entrepreneurial spirit!

Given the importance of the issues discussed so far in this chapter, to discuss now the issue of magic, superstition, and divination (fortune telling) may not seem to be significant. And yet it is. Much of western disdain for Islam is based on the observation of primitive, atavistic religious practices surrounding the graves of Muslim "saints," and of black magic practices as well.

---

80. Ibid., 109.

81. Ibid., 121, note 22, would allow interest in the amount of inflation.

If, in particular, one is exposed to the popular cult which grew up around "marabout" tombs in the Maghreb, one will conclude easily that this religion of Islam is so irrational that it can appeal only to backward people. To what other conclusion would such an observer come if, for instance in Fez, he would perchance stroll into one of those shops where one sells exclusively accessories for practicing black magic. Like little dolls through which one can drive a needle . . . .

Marabouts in Morocco and western Algeria, as everyone knows, are responsible for the fertility of women and farmers' fields and are, of course, very helpful in love affairs as well.

Several successive pilgrimages to certain saints like 'Abd al Salām ibn M'Chich (d. 1228) in the Rif mountains near Tangier or to Moulay Idrīs near Meknes, where the founder of the first Moroccan Muslim dynasty, Idrīs I, is buried—are considered as equaling the merits of, and replacing, the hajj . . . .

These heterodox practices, smacking of Christian cults, crept into Islam in the context of the Sufi movements, mainly in and after the thirteenth century. It is, of course, a fact that Muslim Sufi *ṭuruq* (mystical orders) all encourage a strong personality cult and total submission of the *murīd* (seeker, disciple) under his Sufi guide and teacher. Rightly so, westerners find all this abhorrent.

The idea that, thanks to a family relationship with the Prophet, certain people, the *shurufā'*, enjoyed a special mystical power—*barakah*—is part of this syndrome. It is considered a courtesy vis-à-vis the Prophet (and meritorious because of one's *nīyah jamīlah*) to suppress even reasonable doubts about the lineage of somebody pretending to be a *sharīf* or about the authenticity of a "sacred" tomb.[82]

---

82. Fritz Meier,"Zum vorrang des glaubens und des güten denkens vor dem wahrheitseifer bei den Muslimen," *Oriens* 32, 1990.

Such pious and yet heretical courtesy was also responsible for the development of excessive *mawlūd* ceremonies (for the Prophet Muhammad) which, at least in the Maghrib and sometimes in Turkey, can be painfully reminiscent of Christmas Eve. When will Muslims understand that they are doing a disservice to our beloved Prophet when elevating him to a supernatural being? Is not his merit the higher, the lower his (purely human) status?

How much abuse, all through history, has been made of green turbans! And how much people have let themselves be instrumentalized by the notion of *barakah*! If you still need evidence of this, I suggest a visit to the graves of Idrīs II and Aḥmad Tijānī in Fez, where one can watch tattooed Berber women[83] roll themselves underneath the green cloths covering these tombs so as to better partake of the available *barakah*. Revolting.

If nothing else, the cult of saints proves a popular craving for something sacred that one can touch—in other words: for divine incarnation. Thus, even Muslim populations in formerly Christian territory developed their own ways of producing a cuddly "Baby Jesus" in the form of "saintly" Muslim ascetics, dervishes, and other people of *taṣawwuf*.

This should not be tolerated, since seeking intercession violates one of the most fundamental tenets of Islam. I suggest that the entire Islamic world, in this respect, should adopt the Wahhābī rejection of any cult of saints. Also, in the Wahhābī spirit, we should strive for the elaboration of a *sīrah* of our Prophet that, cleansed from all later legends and attributions of miracles, could be used for contemporary *da'wah*.[84] We owe this to our justified contention that

83. The Islamic prohibition of tattooing (al Bukhārī, 72, hadiths 827 and 830) was entirely ineffective among the Berber tribes in Morocco and Algeria. This also creates feelings of contempt.

84. For details, see Hussein Amin, *Le livre du musulman desemparé* (Paris: 1992), 23-29.

Islam is a sober religion that appeals to emancipated, grown-up people who think. Let us, at any rate, not be put to shame by new works of *sīrah* published by well-meaning non-Muslims.[85]

This lack of indulgence does not mean that we should physically destroy the last resting places of such great personalities as Ibn Shāfi'ī in Cairo or Ibn 'Arabī in Damascus nor the tomb of Eyüp (Ayyūb) Sultan, flag-bearer of the Prophet, on the Golden Horn of Istanbul. Muslims, too, have a history of which to be conscious and proud.

This chapter would not be complete without mentioning another custom that contributes to the ridicule of Muslims in Occidental eyes: divination, mostly (as in Turkey) in the form of "reading the future" from coffee grounds (*fal*). Muslims of all people, considered fatalists, have maintained to this day an extraordinary interest in knowing beforehand what is going to happen. This attempt to play God has been outlawed rigidly by the Qur'an 5:3, together with the consumption of pork. Pork disappeared in the Islamic world; divination did not.

By such recommendations I do not want to create even more fission in the Islamic camp than already visible. Division between Sunni, Shi'a, and Khārijī (Ibāḍī and Mozabite) Muslims, between Mu'tazilah and Ash'arīyah, is bad enough. But how to look through the maze of mystical orders—from Qādirīyah to Aḥmadīyah, from Nakhshbandīyah to Nurculuk? And where to place the Druzes, Alevites, Alawites, Qadiani, and other sects with some Islamic coloring? Not to speak of the many "Islamist," i.e., political liberation movements calling themselves Hamas or Islamic Jihad. And what is the relationship between those of the Ikhwān al Muslimūn or the Tablīgh al Islāmī?

Questions for us Muslims, and even more questions for the outsider who tries to decipher the authentic voice of Islam. The

85. Virgil Ghiorghiu, *La vie de Mahomet* (Paris: 1970); Karen Armstrong, *Muhammad: A Western Attempt to Understand Islam* (London: 1991).

scissions and fissions mentioned above are a tremendous handicap for dialogue, because our potential partners can pick whose views suit them best and can demonize all of us on the basis of the actions of a minority. I suggest that if we want to be taken seriously, we must be heard to speak with one voice, at least on major moral issues like abortion, surrogate motherhood, organ transplantation, and the like.

To be more modest: It would already be a useful step in the right direction if everybody would only speak for those whom he can represent—nobody any more trying to monopolize Islam. This would be easier if the *khilāfah* had not been abolished in 1924 or if the Muslim ummah could since have agreed on a successor.

Even before that date, the initiative of 'Abd al Raḥmān al awākibī (d. 1902) in favor of a Qurayshī *khalīfah* residing in Makkah as a titular head of a federal union of Muslim states, was unrealistic.[86] The father of Muslim secularism, 'Alī 'Abd al Rāziq (d. 1966) even pretended that "the Islamic khalifat does not at all belong to what has been foreseen as a plan by the (Muslim) religion."[87]

After 1924, only once—fifty years later in 1974—a concrete attempt was made to confer the title of *khalīfah* on a Muslim dignitary. During the Second Summit of the Organization of the Islamic Conference (OIC), some heads of state had unsuccessfully offered this honor to the Saudi king, Faysal ibn Sa'ud.

It is, in fact, doubtful whether the appointment of a *khalīfah* would have been a good thing for the Muslim world community since it was, and continues to be, split into now more than 40 states. Under these conditions, a *khalīfah* could not exercise political power. He would rather be reduced to playing a religious role, as

86. 'Abd al Raḥmān al Kawākibī, *Umm al Qurā* (The Mother of Cities), (1899).

87. 'Alī 'Abd al Rāziq, *al Islām wa Uṣūl al Ḥukm* (Cairo: 1925).

sort of a Muslim pope.[88] Even if it were more effective, the OIC itself, founded in Rabat in 1969, should not, and could not, pose as a "*khilāfah* by committee" either.

We have to admit that currently there is simply no one in sight who could fill that vacuum today. But, we should at least remain acutely aware of that vacuum, hoping for a great, charismatic religious leader to reemerge soon: An Ibn Taymīyah or a Niẓām al Mulk of the twenty-first century.

In calling for unity, I do not want to give the impression that there should be Muslim uniformity. There never was and never will be. Nobody would question today that not only the Arabs but also the Persians, the Berbers, the Afghans, and the Turks became "Muslim peoples." But so had the Visigoths of Andalusia. And so have the Indonesians, the Malays, and the Pakistanis. Each of these ethnic entities, while becoming Muslim, maintained many features of their civilization—just as the Arabs, too, in terms of their civilization did not start from scratch with their conversion to Islam. The Islamic calendar in the year 1 after the hijrah did not begin with a cultural "zero hour." As a result, it is easy to distinguish on sight—from a head-gear alone!—Muslims from all the countries mentioned. During an Islamic conference in Cairo, I once counted forty-two different types of hats and turbans worn by Muslim men from all over the world.

This observation carries a lesson: When today thousands of Europeans and Americans, whites and nonwhites, enter Islam their conversion may entirely change their outlook on life and behavior, but they remain Frenchmen, Englishmen, Swiss, Spaniards, Canadians, or Germans in other important ways. Each one speaks his own national language, looks at the world slightly

---

88. I share this view with Azizah Y. al-Hibri, "Islamic Constitution and the Concept of Democracy," *Case Western Reserve Journal of Islamic Law*, no. 24 (1992): 16, note 66.

differently. Each one has gone through a slightly different system of education.

In short: An Islam with an American and a European coloring is emerging side by side with the Islam of Maghribean or Egyptian coloring. Not a "German Islam"—God forbid!—but an Islam in Germany, not an American Islam—but an Islam in the United States. This new development will help us to see more clearly what features of the Islam we are familiar with is part of its essence, and which of its features are merely a matter of Arab or other civilizations.

Non-Arab pilgrims, not only from sub-Saharan Africa, when visiting Makkah and al Madinah, might at times get the impression that the proud Arabs they encounter there consider themselves a "chosen people"—not unlike the Jewish tribes. If this were so, it would be humanly understandable and pardonable. And yet it would be wrong.

Islam does not encourage tribal (nationalistic) solidarity over Muslim solidarity (Qur'an 28:15 and 49:13), because nationalism misguides people into helping their own kind in an unjust cause. The latter verse could not be more unambiguous: "We . . . have made you into nations and tries, so that you might come to know each other. Verily, the noblest of you in the sight of God is the one who is most deeply conscious of Him . . . ." Thus no Muslim should disqualify any other for whatever undertaking, even ijtihad, only on the basis of his ethnic background.

It is quite another story that Muslims are urged to obey Allah and His Messenger (Qur'an 3:32, 8:46, 24:52 and 54, 33:36, and 47:33), the first of all Muslims (Qur'an 6:14 and 163), and the model to emulate (Qur'an 33:21). To emulate Muhammad may take the form of young Europeans dressing, growing their beard, eating and brushing their teeth exactly as Muhammad had done. In doing so, they emulate not only the Prophet but also the civilization in the Hijāz of the Quraysh of the seventh century C.E.

The effect of this approach is obvious: Islam is portrayed as a religion for and by Arabs, and these young European Muslims tend to become part of a subculture with folkloristic coloring. For Islamic *da'wah*, these effects are detrimental, to put it mildly.

All along this chapter has been focusing on issues that are crucial for the western perception of Islam, i.e., on issues of communication. I hope not to insult anybody when stating that the Muslim world seems to be particularly inept to portray itself attractively. An unshaven Yasir Arafat with a pistol on his belt on television is about the best propaganda anti-Arab forces could wish to have, and that for free. Dignified Arab shaykhs have not been able to counteract the slapstick image of the lascivious old Arab, with abducted blond women in his tent and an oil well nearby.

These and other stereotypes of the oversexed, treacherous, trigger-happy, and dumb Arab can be found in virtually each and every Hollywood film playing in the Orient. These optically created prejudices are of course immediately transferred to the entire Islamic world. It is therefore an understatement to say that the Muslim world at large is suffering from a monumental public relations deficit. What MBC, based in London, does in Arabic should therefore be done extensively on British, French, German, Spanish, Italian, and American television.

Undeniably, there is quite an amount of well-meaning Islamic literature shipped into western countries from Muslim sources. Alas, most of this material is ineffective not only because of low quality paper, faulty English, and incredible amounts of printing mistakes. This kind of *da'wah* effort suffers even more by its approach: Usually it preaches to the converted.

How can I convince somebody by quoting "God's word" from the Qur'an as long as he is not yet convinced of the existence of a God Who might speak?

All of the typical ways of proving the existence of a divine Creator to a Muslim are usually ineffective when tried on an Occidental

CHAPTER 7

The Task ahead of Us: What a Task!

In order to rejuvenate the religion of Islam, and in order to improve its image in the interest of *da'wah,* some or all of the changes proposed in the previous chapter must be realized, soon.

I am not the first one to suggest this, but am much indebted, in addition to Muhammad Asad,[89] to constructive reformers like Jamāl al Bannā (b. 1920),[90] Hamīd Sulaymān,[91] and Ḥusayn Amīn—my former colleague as ambassador to Algeria—whose courageous book *Sabīl al Muslim al Ḥazīn ila Muqtaḍa al Sulūk fi al Qarn al 'Ishrīn* (1983),[92] should be heeded by everyone in the field. Nor am I sufficiently competent to do more than lay some of the groundwork for the task ahead of us. Its achievement requires teamwork between knowledgeable and devoted Muslim scholars from all fields of science, working without political or financial constraints.

And what a task this is, because the recommendations of the previous chapter presuppose, for their realization, fundamental changes in attitudes and approach that must be grounded on a sound doctrinal basis.

We do not want to give Islam a cosmetic face-lift so as to make it more attractive. We want to make Islam more vital, dynamic,

89. Muḥammad Asad, *This Law of Ours and Other Essays* (Gibraltar: 1987), 1-71.

90. Jamāl al Banna, *al Barnamaj al Islāmī* (Cairo: 1991).

91. Ḥamīd Sulaymān, *Alghām fi Ṭarīq al Ṣaḥwah al Islāmīyah* (Cairo: 1990).

92. Its French version, *Le Livre du musulman desemparé*, appeared in Paris in 1992.

relevant, and therefore attractive by scrubbing away foreign elements, rust, and veneer. In particular, this presupposes that we stop confusing:

- the religion and the civilization of Islam,
- its essential and marginal aspects,
- tradition and *taqlīd,*
- sound and fabricated hadiths,
- Shari'ah and *fiqh,* and
- Qur'an and Sunnah.

In this context, it will be decisive to develop better criteria for judging what about traditional Islam is, and what is not, an integral part of this great religion, what is essential and what is marginal.

Perhaps the most striking example of civilization posing as religion is the partial or total veiling of women's faces. Some can still be found in Jeddah veiling themselves four-fold, almost blinding their vision and making themselves hazards to motorized traffic. In Beni Isguen or El-Ateuf near Ghardaia (M'Zab, southern Algeria) women consider themselves indecently dressed unless their face is covered—except for one eye. And even mummified that way, they turn to the wall if a man comes walking their way.[93] In Yemen, one can still encounter women covering their nose and mouth with a leather mask.

When I discussed this fact with the former Shaykh al Azhar, Gādd al Ḥaqq 'Alī Gādd al Ḥaqq, in Cairo in 1989, he stated that such practices were "not Islamic, but also not entirely un-Islamic," which I took to mean that certain customs can gain sort of a common law legitimacy through mere usage over a long period of time.

93. Aicha Daddi Abdoun, *Sociologie et Historie des algeriens ibadites* (Ghardaia: 1977).

To such an interpretation, my answer is that *customs cannot possibly abrogate Qur'anic freedoms conferred on women.*

Thus, there is a case for separating religion and civilization. Only if we can peel away the many layers of civilizationary, local lacquer can pristine Islam, like a freshly polished jewel, become universally relevant everywhere in our time: As undiluted monotheism, belief in a living transcendental and immanent God, and unreserved submission to Him.

The newsletter of the German section of the Muslim League, *DML-Rundbrief,* habitually publishes translations from the question-and-answer columns of the Saudi periodicals *Arab News* and *al Musilmoon.* Not the answers but the questions are startling! Here is a selection of what bothers certain Muslims in Saudi Arabia:

- Must I repeat ritual washing if I touched a non-Muslim?
- Is music legitimate for a Muslim?
- Can a Muslim study foreign law?
- In which localities is it forbidden to say *al salāmu 'alaykum*?
- Does the coloring of one's hair invalidate ritual washing? Does smoking have this effect?
- Can a Muslim accept gold crowns for the protection of his teeth?
- Can a Muslim drink alcohol-free beer?
- Must a Muslim avoid cosmetics containing alcohol or substances, like gelatin, obtained from pigs?
- Is it Islamic to be left-handed?
- Can one offer a copy of the Qur'an to a non-Muslim?
- Is it allowed to celebrate one's birthday?

Indeed, I found no better way of presenting the issue of separating marginal aspects from the essentials.

My answer to such Talmudic questions would have been: I sincerely wish I only had your problems! And the counter-questions:

What kind of God do you think Allah is—a picayune book-keeper? What kind of religion do you think Islam is—a haven for trivial lawyers?

Alas, we see a trend to the contrary, even among some new converts to Islam for whom brushing their teeth by means of a *siwāk*, putting on their right shoes first, and cutting their mustache correctly may become important in itself, and out of all proportion. We all prefer to recognize Muslims rather by character traits like their tolerance, generosity, charity, patience, compassion, and zeal in prayer? Or don't we?

As I mentioned earlier, the spirit of *taqlīd* is still with us, even while the door to new interpretation (*bāb al ijtihād*) may be wide open in theory.

In this context, we can be sure to have the blessing of the founders of the four schools of law (*madhāhib*). They were conscious of the fact that legal ordinances start leading their own life the moment they have been promulgated. No generation of jurists can foresee, for all future generations to come, which problems will arise and which aspects of Qur'anic norms will become relevant for their resolution. That laws may change with the passage of time may well be considered a fundamental principle of Islamic jurisprudence. Therefore, each generation finds itself in the situation of the first generation of Muslims. Before any schools of law, compilations of hadith, or even the idea of Sunnah ever existed, these early Muslims had to act according to their best knowledge and judgment. And so must we. Let us not be afraid of our own courage.

Any "modern" Muslim will be full of admiration for what our forefathers achieved in collecting, sifting, compiling, and classifying the traditions concerning what Muhammad said, did, or tolerated. Also, no Muslim may deny that the Prophet did not only transmit but explained the divine message received by him, even through his behavior.

At the same time, it is a truism to state that Sunni, Shi'i, and Ibāḍī Muslims do not honor the same compilations of *aḥādīth,* for each group holds onto its own set, which is not fully compatible with the others. And, of course, while we know how much pious scholars like al Bukhārī and Muslim battled to weed out forged *aḥādīth*, who can be sure that they were entirely successful?

Doubts are justified, because the six orthodox hadith collections were all assembled by the same criteria. In particular, out of sheer veneration of the Companions of the Prophet, *isnād* (chain of transmission) and *maṭn* (text) critique did not go as far as it would have if modern linguistic and sociohistorical analysis had been applied.

Given the fact that tens of thousands of fabricated hadiths circulated within two centuries of the Prophet's death, we simply have to admit that the Sunnah is not as reliable as we would all wish it to be. Let us be cruelly sober: Someone clever and ruthless enough to fabricate the *matn* of a hadith—be it for political or "pious" reasons—would he not be clever and ruthless enough to also fabricate its *isnād* ?

And do we not all virtually smell that something is fishy with certain political *aḥādīth,* in particular those favoring 'Alī, or Mu'āwīyah, or men over women. Do we not feel more "comfortable" with the realism of traditions by 'Ā'isha and smile about some reported from the somewhat childish perspective of the lovable Abū Hurayrah?

Competent scholars, must—and not like Fatima Mernissi[94]—reestablish not with an ax but with a surgeon's precision instruments, what is *ṣaḥīḥ* (correct) and what is *ḍa'īf* (weak). If we cannot manage this task, more and more European and American Mus-

94. This Moroccan author is not competent in Islamic history, philosophy, and theology. Yet she dabbles in all these fields. See, as an example, Fatima Mernissi, *Le harem politique, Le Prophet et les femmes* (Paris: 1987).

lims, like Roger Garaudy, will be tempted to base their argumentation exclusively on the text of the Qur'an.[95]

It is equally important to restore to the concept of Shari'ah its original meaning, which denotes Qur'anic norms only. Thus, the term *fiqh* would be reserved to denote the entire body of Islamic law and jurisprudence that developed on the bases of the Qur'an and Sunnah.

This is not an idle undertaking, but rather an attempt to desacralize some of the enormous legal material left from the Middle Ages as a first step for true ijtihad. It is an appeal repetitive of the one made by Muhammad Asad already more than thirty years ago, namely, to distinguish between the small number of eternal and unchangeable divine decrees found in the indisputable text of the Qur'an from the bulk of rules and ordinances, man-made and based on less secure textual material, found in the legal treatises of venerable *fuqahā'*.[96]

This brings us to the last important point in clarifying doctrine: The status relationship between the Qur'an and Sunnah.

One would think that there was no problem, given the indisputable fact that the Qur'an is God's own word, which, upon revelation, was recorded in writing immediately and faithfully, while the Sunnah—even a *ḥadīth qudsī*—is based on texts, formulated by the Prophet, and committed to writing centuries later. In view of this, it seems preposterous that anyone should conceive of certain Qur'anic verses being derogated by the Sunnah. Yet this view is maintained by some ulama.

Perhaps the most illustrative and pertinent case in point is the opinion held by some that *zinā* (adultery) should carry the death

---

95. Typical for this trend are Roger Garaudy's booklets *For an Islam of the XXth Century* (Paris: 1985) and *L'Islam vivant* (Alger: 1986).

96. Muḥammad Asad, *State and Government in Islam* (1st ed. 1961; 2d ed. Gibraltar: 1980), 11-17.

penalty by stoning (as in the Bible), even while the Qur'an specifically orders one hundred lashes only (17:32; 24:2).[97] How can a *faqīh* (jurist), on the basis of hadith,[98] ever dare to substitute death for flogging once God has spoken unambiguously? This never would have happened if those sciences connected with the Islamic religious law had maintained the obvious difference in status between the primary source of Islam, the Qur'an, and its indispensable secondary source, the Sunnah.

Some, if not all, of the undertakings suggested in this chapter will probably run into heavy "flack." To be expected is resistance by *fuqahā'* who are rightfully afraid of *bid'ah* (innovation)—while knowing so well what constitutes *bid'ah ḥasanah* ("good innovation")! These are the people, of course, who quite innocently helped the Islamic world into its later state of mental rigidity with a typical bunker mentality stemming from the period when Islam had to be defended against the overwhelming odds of colonization.

Surely, nobody will openly defend nowadays the notion that the *bāb al ijtihād* is still closed (if ever it had been). But few are the contemporary ulama outside Shi'ism and Sufism who dare go through that open door . . . and censorship, officially or self-imposed, does the rest.

Take a look at the rich documentation available on the intellectual development of Islam all through its fourteen centuries.[99] I cannot believe that the last chapters of these books will remain their concluding chapter for long. But given the situation just mentioned,

---

97. See in great detail Si Boubakeur Hamza, *Le Coran*, Vol. 2 (Paris: 1985), commentary to 24:2 and Hussein Amin, op. cit., 50.

98. The relevant ahadith are to be found in *Ṣaḥīḥ al Bukhārī*, Book 63 on Divorce, no. 31, and Book 82, on Punishment, nos. 807-10.

99. M. M. Sharif, ed., *A History of Muslim Philosophy*, 2 vols. (Wiesbaden: 1963/1966); Majid Fakhry, *A History of Islamic Philosophy*, 2d ed. (London and New York: 1983); Henry Corbin, *History of Islamic Philosophy* (London: 1993).

the liveliness of intellectual life necessary for Islamic rejuvenation will probably be found rather in places like Los Angeles, Washington, Leicester, Oxford, Cologne, and Paris than in traditional centers of Muslim learning.

It is, therefore, not far-fetched to expect the intellectual and spiritual revivification of Islam in the twenty-first century to be kindled and propelled from research done by qualified Muslim thinkers working outside *dār al Islām.*

But Allah knows best, and in Him we trust, and to Him shall we all return.